TEN BEST STEPS TEACHING YOURSELF TO SWIM SAFELY AND EFFICIENTLY

TEACH YOURSELF TO SWIM
e-Book Series
IN ONE MINUTE STEPS

"Start at home and easily transfer these familiar motor skills to the shallow end of a pool or lake on a weekend or summer trip"

By

DR. PETE ANDERSEN

http://www.LearnToSwimProgram.com

http://bit.ly/FaceBook-LearnToSwimProgram

http://bit.ly/YouTube-LearnToSwimProgram

https://www.Pinterest.com/LearnToSwimProg

www.SwimVideoCoach.com

www.YouTube.com/SwimVideoCoach

www.TeachYourselfToSwim.com

Your comments and www.Amazon.com reviews are welcome.

JOIN OUR MISSION TO HELP SAVE MORE LIVES!!!

Enjoy and pass along what you learn to others

Trius Publishing, P.O. Box 600801, San Diego, CA 92160

TEN BEST STEPS TEACHING YOURSELF TO SWIM SAFELY AND EFFICIENTLY

Copyright © 2014 by Dr. Pete Andersen
Published in the United States by:

Trius Publishing, P.O. Box 600801, San Diego, CA 92160
www.TriusPublishing.com and www.DrPeteAndersen.com

All rights reserved. No part of this e-book may be reproduced by any mechanical, photographic, or electronic process, or in the form of an audio recording nor may it be stored in a retrieval system, transmitted, or otherwise be copied for public or private use—other than for "fair use" as brief quotations embodied in articles and reviews without prior written permission of the author and publisher.

The author of this book does not dispense medical advice or prescribe the use of any technique as a form of treatment for physical or mental problems without the advice of a physician, either directly or indirectly. The intent of the author is only to offer information of a general nature to help you in your quest for performance improvement. In the event you use any of the information in this book for yourself or to help others is your constitutional right, the author and publisher assume no responsibility for your actions.

Paperback ISBN: 978-0-9820248-6-7

ASIN: B00TXWW284

List of paperback / Kindle books and DVD sets in the

TEACH YOURSELF TO SWIM series -
IN ONE MINUTE STEPS [or Your Child] TO SWIM

ISBN # / ASIN #   Title

ISBN # / ASIN #	Title
978-0-9820248-7-4 B00TSV32EC	TEACH YOURSELF OR YOUR CHILD TO SWIM AT HOME WITHOUT A POOL
978-0-9820248-2-9 B00TXWW284	TEN BEST STEPS TEACHING YOURSELF TO SWIM SAFELY AND EFFICIENTLY
978-0-9820248-8-1 B01CYYTQPO	FLOATING RELAXED
978-0-9820248-9-8 B01CZK84FK	FREESTYLE WITH BREATHING
978-0-9899468-0-3 B01CZK8971	USING YOUR OWN FEEDBACK
978-0-9899468-1-0 B01CZLEH2S	USING SIX NEW TEACHING METHODS
978-0-9899468-2-7 B01CZLERQY	BACKSTROKE THE EASY WAY
978-0-9899468-3-4 B01CZM0KU0	WATER SAFETY CONCERNS IN OTHER ENVIRONMENTS
978-0-9899468-4-1 B01CZMM846	WATER SAFETY RESTING SKILLS
978-0-9899468-5-8 B01D0EO3VO	IN DEEP WATER WITHOUT FEAR
978-0-9899468-6-5 B01D0FA7S6	SHALLOW TO DEEP WATER PROGRESSION
978-0-9899468-7-2 B01D0FABI2	ELEMENTARY BACKSTROKE FOR SAFETY
978-0-9899468-8-9 B01D0FP9HU	BREASTSTROKE THE EASY WAY
978-0-9899468-9-6 B01D0G7VDY	ADVANCED WORKOUT SKILLS
978-0-9820248-3-6	Active Lifestyle (3 DVD set 5 hours 37 minutes)
978-0-9820248-4-3	Parents, Grandparents, Beginners, Non-Swimmers, Instructors (4 DVD set 7 hours 24 minutes)
978-0-9820248-5-0	Competitor Masters, Senior Olympians, Triathletes, Age-Group Swimmers (2 DVD set 3 hours 21 minutes)

TBD/ASIN	Ten Best Steps Teaching Yourself to Swim Safely and Efficiently (1 DVD 1 hour 15 minutes)

Series of single DVD disks of the same content as the e-books is being completed as of this printing. They will be available on Amazon and my shopping cart for under $10.

See fast link below.

You can order from

www.Amazon.com/Books

www.Amazon.com/Videos

OR   order directly from the website

www.LearnToSwimProgram.com

shopping cart using the fast link:

http://bit.ly/1NdevtV

Most of these are under $10 to get you started.

Author's Personal Message of Introduction

In August of 2010 I heard a news report of nine related African-American teens that drowned in the Arkansas River trying to rescue each other. My emotion immediately shifted to thinking how I would feel losing one of my six kids or now thirteen grandchildren.

I sat down in a chair and cried for about twenty minutes. And then I got mad thinking how could teenagers not even know how to make a human chain to interlock wrists to wade in and rescue someone in a current?

That thought prompted another, "How can we teach people to swim in rural and low income areas where there is no pool or an experienced instructor like to me to show them how they can teach themselves to swim?" For the past 50 plus years since I learned to teach swimming as a high school freshman and went on to earn my B.S. and M.S. teaching degrees in health and physical education at Indiana University I have monitored the evolution of swimming instruction.

At Indiana I was also a 5-time NCAA Division I All-American coached by the legend Doc Counsilman who later coached Mark Spitz and our winningest 1964 and 1976 U.S. Men's Olympic Swimming Teams and a string of six NCAA Championships.

From Doc and my teaching degrees I learned how to apply all the physics principles to learn to swim instruction. At the same time to finance my graduate degree I was a Director of Aquatics for Country Clubs and a large Chicago suburban high school and park district of 80,000 people. I directed and trained all our high school student instructors to teach swimming to our community grade school children in our Saturday morning and summer swim school programs.

Before I started in my first teaching and head coaching position I had already been teaching swimming for ten years. But after four more years gaining valuable director experience running large programs I felt I needed more knowledge.

I went back to graduate school to earn my Ph.D. in psychology of learning principles with emphasis in behavioral and educational psychology and statistical analysis. I completed a three year program in two years because I was allowed to collect dissertation data while I was attending classes.

Another reason was because my wife at the time and I had triplet boys born three months into my program to add to my three-year-old son. Between helping at home bathe, feed, and change diapers, and going to classes and teaching classes as a grad assistant I only got an average of four hours sleep.

With my swimming pedigree the University put me in charge of teaching most of the college swimming courses. And for my dissertation I tested our 1972 U.S. Men's Olympic Swim Team and six of the top ten NCAA Division I teams.

All throughout my degree programs it was impressed on all students to embrace professional growth - to keep learning. Over the years teaching thousands to swim and hundreds to be quality instructors I found that my students taught me!

I would change my method or cue and see how they would respond to learn that skill faster. Later now in my book and videos I have introduced six new teaching methods no other instructor or program is using.

I had already added physics principles and now added psychology of learning principles from my Ph.D. I've learned that no other instructor in the world has achieved. Coupled with having swum and been a 5-time All-American mentored by the greatest swim coach of all time I am blessed with very good skills.

Using these skills and my desire to prove my system of easy-to-master one minute steps gets faster longer-lasting results, I got back into competitive swimming with the U.S. Masters Swimming. It took six years of training to set my first World Record, and since I've always been in the top 10 in the U.S. and FINA World Rankings for my age group. I have also achieved 21 Senior Olympic Summer Games Championships Gold Medals with records to match.

I like to tell people it's not like I'm a man telling a woman how to have a baby. I practice and prove what I teach every day. My proven results and ability means I know how to correctly demonstrate and teach the correct visual, verbal, and most important kinesthetic or feeling cues with imagery techniques to speed up the learning process.

My system is now proven to get faster longer-lasting results because it follows a system of sequential steps to make it easier for the brain to learn. The imagery cues I use are universal to children and adults like floating level as an air mattress, or reaching over a barrel or a ball to get your hand catch and arm rotation correct for example.

In the summer of 2010 when those nine teens drowned I took action and sat down to write up a sequential curriculum for all the strokes. I also wanted to write in simple terms to explain how never out-of-date physics and psychology of learning principles would be applied so people could learn to teach themselves to swim with my correct pictures demonstrating the skills.

This would really help save more lives especially in rural and low income areas or when people had large families. I reasoned that 1) learning to swim is a necessity and the only sport that has the potential to save your life, and 2) water has a way of finding you when you are least prepared that can lead to panic and a tragic result.

Eventually I became an expert in drowning prevention and swimming instruction to do radio interviews all over the U.S. My book and the only complete video curriculum instructional series in the world to include all the strokes plus water safety concerns in unfamiliar places were published.

To my surprise thinking that all major swim programs would embrace my work based on physics and psychology of learning as "the new science of swimming instruction" for professional growth to upgrade swimming instruction and the universal mission to save more lives that has not happened.

All the major organizations have proved very protective and unwilling to change. Therein lays the most significant problem why unintentional drowning deaths have not declined in the last few decades.

In my analysis getting all my fairly reliable statistics from the Atlanta based Centers for Disease Control and Prevention or CDC there are still on average ten unintentional drowning deaths each day in the U.S. and many more in other countries. The most likely reason is there are no pools or experienced instructors.

There are cultural issues and myths to overcome. As reported by the CDC 70% of blacks and 60% of Hispanics do not know how to swim. The worst myth is that blacks have heavier bones and smaller lungs and cannot float. What a lie that is!

In the 1000's I've taught to swim I've only had two black males who were body builders with only 6% body fat that were negatively buoyant. But I still taught them how to swim.

If the mother does not know how to swim their child has only a 13% chance of learning how to swim. But if a child learns to swim before the age of four they have an 88% chance of surviving a water accident.

Now you can see the importance I place on teaching parents how to start teaching their babies to swim at home without a pool at 2-18 months when they bathe them. This process is no harder than teaching their kids to learn and improve any backyard sports skill to transfer to the playing field or court.

I try to change all that at home without a pool using their kitchen sink, dressing mirror, mattress, and a bathtub. Now they can get familiar with all the basic physical motor patterns at home without fear of drowning.

Then when they learn at their own pace and feel confident they can transfer those same familiar skills to the shallow end of a pool or lake where they can stand up. I even teach people how to float with their mouth open to make a better air lock with their nose and how to use goggles to see the pool bottom to place their feet and stand up!

When a lot of people live in rural areas or have large families and cannot afford pool admission or lessons my "TEACH YOURSELF TO SWIM" system helps solves this growing problem to help save more lives.

Rather than waste any more time with other swimming instructional organizations and programs I have elected to use technology and social media to reach out to people in need to save them time and money and frustration. All my content is available on Amazon, select bookstores and swim outlet stores, and my website www.LearnToSwimProgram.com or shop directly using this link http://bit.ly/1NdevtV

I've learned that kids like adults don't like to waste their time when they are not learning from young inexperienced instructors who cannot demonstrate or teach with correct methods and cues because they are not being taught how to teach by the organizations. They make certification a joke in the U.S., but not in Australia or New Zealand where I have visited and had meetings with their organization directors. You have to prove your ability to teach before they will certify you.

The result is that most of the kids taking lessons today never master their rhythmical breathing to swim continuously any distance to save their life. Even their floating skills are poor. And worse, they never learn about wave actions, currents, marine life, and hypothermia to avoid risks.

The #1 reason why people unintentionally drown is because they overestimate their swimming ability. Most learn in a clear heated pool with goggles. And once they pass a minimal test they are cleared to have fun and go off the diving boards in the deep well. So they think they are good enough swimmers because they can make it from the diving board to the ladder.

But that won't help them in an ocean rip or river current or fast moving stream in a flood. Boys and young men are the worst at getting their macho ego involved to overestimate their ability. So I created the mental skills swim test.

Sit down in a chair and close your eyes. Now imagine swimming out into a lake 100 yards where you cannot see the bottom and the water is only 70 degrees. That's only the length of a football field. Okay now rest a bit and swim back.

If you took a gasp or deeper than normal breathing cycle, or your heart rate started to increase slightly, then you are not as good a swimmer as you think you are. Kids on swim teams would have no problem doing that.

Of the ten people who unintentionally drown each day two are children generally under the age of four. But the other eight are adults! What percentage of those eight adults probably took lessons as kids? So why has the number not been declining.

Could it be that large organizations are not willing to upgrade their swimming teaching methods and cues to reflect the new science applying physics and psychology of learning principles?

That is what I am all about and have proven results so you can benefit from in the contents of my work producing a book and video curriculum series. I believe I can teach you better on your own TV or downloading my chapters to your tablet to take to the pool or lake than any young inexperienced teacher.

And now for the first time I have created a series of e-books, paperbacks, and video disks devoted to only one smaller part of the curriculum at a time to make it even more affordable for everyone to teach themselves. My system of easy-to-master one minute steps is embedded in each product's content so you can get faster longer-lasting results, save money, time, and most important improve the overall safety of your family.

After you invest and use any of my products I'd like to learn your comments. You are also going to get a series of three "fast-start" tutorials for free you can forward to all your friends and family on emails and links to the tutorials on your social media. Together we can help save more lives.

Sincerely,

Pete Andersen, Ph.D.

For free swim tips www.LearnToSwimProgram.com/Swim-Tips or use this link http://bit.ly/1NdevtV to shop

*** FREE BONUS OFFER ***

Get valuable FREE content. Forward a copy of your Amazon Kindle book receipt to: drpete@LearnToSwimProgram.com OR ... complete the easy form on my website www.LearnToSwimProgram.com/Subscribe OR ...

Scan the code or text or voice mail your name and email to 1-858-886-9820
and
I will give you my download to my

Best Selling e-book valued at $9.97
"Teach Yourself or Your Kids to Swim
at Home Without a Pool"

AND

My popular nine page article
"Tips to Prevent Drowning"

AND

Get three valuable "Fast-Start" tutorials & podcasts

AND

Please provide your book review. Get the fast link from

http://www.LearnToSwimProgram.com/Amazon-Reviews

Find us on ...

http://bit.ly/FaceBook-LearnToSwimProgram

http://bit.ly/YouTube-LearnToSwimProgram

https://www.Pinterest.com/LearnToSwimProg

www.LinkedIn.com/In/DrPeteAndersen

www.Twitter.com/DrPeteAndersen

To give me permission to send you
VALUABLE FREE content, or
go to leave a comment or ask your question:

http://www.LearnToSwimProgram.com/Contact-Form

and submit the easy form

****

To find out how to achieve all your
swimming strokes, water safety
and more, go to:

http://www.LearnToSwimProgram.com/Resources

The following contents are listed for you to choose
your level of interest.

Would you benefit from more quality **FREE CONTENT** tips, webinars, and videos to get faster longer lasting results?

Could your Age-Group or Masters Swimming Teams benefit from a $3,000 - $7,500 easy "turn-key" program **FUNDRAISER**?

Would you like to be rewarded for recommending our quality books/DVDs to your family, relatives, friends, neighbors, co-workers, teammates, using your e-mail and social media? Then be sure to sign up for our **AFFILIATES** program? It's easy.

Would you like to continue improving your water safety knowledge and swimming skills in a monthly **GROUP MEMBERSHIP** that meets every other week, gives you more resources, and can get all your questions answered?

Do you desire All-American level **PERSONAL COACHING** to take your skills and fitness to the next level with Skype?

Would your organization, association, corporation, or team benefit from one of my professional instructional **CLINICS**?

Would you like to join our mission to save more lives by qualifying to become an **AMBASSADOR** and enjoy getting valuable discounts on books, DVDs, clinics, group membership, and personal coaching?

Imagine enjoying swimming better with family and friends. It's easy with my easy-to-master one minute steps system.

Imagine saving your money and time and getting faster longer lasting results from a pro instructor! Then if you take local lessons you'll get more out of them.

To find out how to achieve all these things and more, go to:

http://www.LearnToSwimProgram.com/Resources

TABLE OF CONTENTS

	3	List of paperback books and DVDs in series
	5	Author's Personal Message of Introduction
	11	Free bonus offer
	15	Personal guarantee and disclaimer
Step 1	17	Kitchen sink progressive sequence
Step 2	22	Dressing mirror progressive sequence
Step 3	27	Mattress progressive sequence
Step 4	31	Bath tub progressive sequence
Step 5	36	Observe pool health & safety signs and depth markings
Step 6	41	Transfer home skills to shallow end of a pool or lake
Step 7	64	Learn how to stand up from neutral floating position
Step 8	67	Arms stroking progressive sequence
Step 9	87	Standing breathing progressive skills sequence
Step 10	91	Swimming and breathing progressive sequence

Personal guarantee and disclaimer

1. MY PERSONAL GUARANTEE AND DISCLAIMER

If you follow my prescribed sequence of steps and practice enough to master each step, you will learn how to swim. For the videos you have 30 days unconditional guarantee from the date of shipment. If you are not committed to learning and practicing, then I would prefer you defer your investment or gift someone in need.

This guarantee is null and void if you are physically and mentally unable to read and/or perform any or several of the skills due to obesity, joint flexibility, injury, deformity, muscle weakness, sprains or strains, or mental condition.

I am not a medical doctor prescribing medical advice. I have a Ph.D. in how we learn motor skills based on psychological principles. From my personal experience, I may explain how I avoid swimmer's ear and fungus infections simply by drying out the outer ear canal with toilet paper on my little finger. This personal practice is not dispensing medical advice.

What you choose to take from this book is at your own direction. What knowledge and skills you choose to share with other people is your right, and I encourage you to help save more lives.

2. THANK YOU FOR TAKING ACTION

It's never too late to improve your lifelong swimming skills. It's easy to believe that unintentional drowning and near drowning happens to the other person. But if you watch the news, you probably have learned about someone in your area who has drowned in the last two years.

I want you to be completely satisfied with the content of this book and/or the videos. You can search on Amazon and find that there is no instructional swimming video <u>series</u> available. There are competitive coaching technique videos which is entirely different from my instructional series.

This book benefits the active lifestyle, parent and grandparent, competitive Masters, Senior Olympians, and triathletes as well as the non-swimmer or novice and inefficient. Instructors benefit by learning new teaching methods and cues that get fast results and save more lives.

You purchased this book to improve your swimming efficiency. You will need to continue to take action to learn each and every step in the sequence for this to be effective for you. As you master each small step you will feel a sense of accomplishment and be motivated and challenged to learn more in the next step. Build your support network by telling your family and friends what you know and are doing.

I have coached All-Americans and know that coaches like to tweak the fine points, but sometimes neglect the imbedded fundamental motor patterns that cause the confusion and prevent improvement in efficient technique to swim farther and faster. Not all great coaches are also great teachers. The psychology of learning in my six teaching methods plays a greater role than the simple application of physics principles.

Use your feeling of reward to build your confidence and motivation to learn all that you can from each of these steps. Being able to say that you know how to swim is not enough. You must also be able to say with clarity that you are comfortable swimming other strokes and in all kinds of aquatic environments by knowing the action and force of water.

Step 1 Kitchen sink progressive sequence

Fundamental Home Preparation Steps
to build motor skills, mind control and feedback

You can learn a lot at home to save time and money on beginner lessons. Your brain must connect associational neurons to complete motor patterns. These take time to form and research evidence suggests this kind of home practice in between lessons also helps learning.

My point is why not do these first before you start to take lessons so that you can get more out of your paid lesson time? Or, why not teach yourself and your kids these fundamentals just like you teach them how to throw and catch a ball to develop those early skills?

If you are an adult with an intense fear of drowning, then in the privacy of your home you can use your mind to overcome your fears without embarrassment. I have never learned of any adult that drowned in their kitchen sink. It's pretty tough to put your face in the water and want to inhale water. But if you can relax with both feet on the ground and put only your face in the water for 10-20 seconds, you are well on your way to getting your mind to control your body parts to swim.

3. FACE UNDERWATER - IN CUPPED HANDS

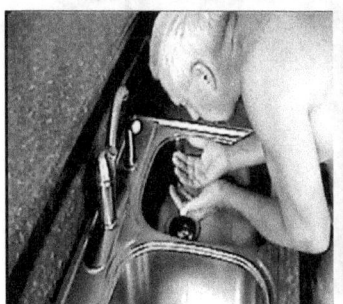 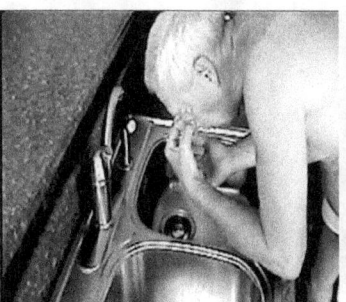 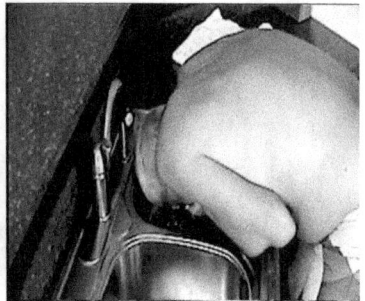

To overcome your fears and use your mind to control those fears about putting your head in the water, I use a kitchen sink so that you can lower just your face into the water, pinch your nose, and start to open your mouth. The water will not rush in, fill your lungs, and drown you. To my knowledge, no one has ever drowned in their kitchen sink. You have an adult brain, use it to sense and control your body parts.

To swim efficiently, you must learn to put your face in the water to float level on top of the water. Being relaxed and in control to float is highly important to your overall success. Now is the time to use your mind to control your body. With practice you will become familiar with putting your face in the water. Your intense fear will be replaced by a positive easy relaxed feeling that becomes your new behavior. This is mind control and behavioral conditioning.

Fill your kitchen sink about two thirds full and use your left hand to pinch your nose. Lower your face into your right hand right just below the water. While your face is submerged with your eyes, nose and mouth hold your breath counting for 10-20 seconds.

4. FINGER IN MOUTH

Repeat putting your face underwater and holding your breath. Take your underwater hand and use your index finger to insert into your open mouth and make a few circles.

As you focus on doing this keep in mind that the water is not rushing in to your lungs. An inverted glass submerged in water won't let the water rush in. You are making a better airlock in your nose by keeping your mouth open. This may be opposite to what major swim programs will tell you to do, but is exactly what every accomplished swimmer does - keeping their mouths open in the water.

 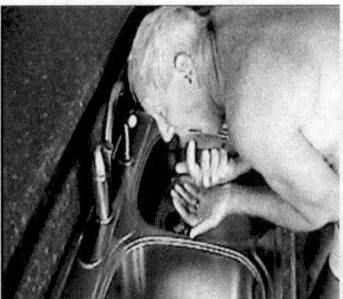 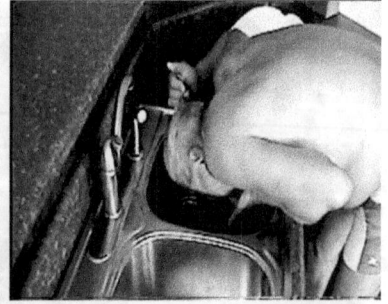

Of course you will not exhale or inhale while you do this. You must also focus on the feeling of your eyes and nose in the water. This may seem uncomfortable to you at first, but mastering this simple skill will pay dividends for you in learning how to swim faster in the succeeding steps that will follow.

By keeping your mouth open and making a better airlock in your nose, you keep water from going up your nose to tickle those tiny hairs. If you close your mouth, those hairs get tickled and subconsciously tell your brain, "You idiot! Are you trying to drown me? Get my head above water." With that you pick your head up which drives your legs and hips down so you have to try to climb out of the water in a state of panic and go nowhere but to exhaustion.

The goal is to imagine yourself floating level keeping your head down to swim over the top of the water like a water ski.

5. SLOWLY EXHALE BUBBLES

Repeat putting your face back down in the water. With your mouth open blow bubbles and feel them float up from your mouth, around and over your cheeks. This is the start of your very first kinesthetic cue to feel an event. Subtle cues are important. For example, a wrong cue to exhale as if you were blowing out a candle encourages you to blow out tiny bubbles that take too much time.

Instead, you need to keep your mouth open and relaxed to blow out and feel large bubbles go up and over your cheeks. Then you can expel 20% of the air out of your lungs quickly, and not disrupt your breathing air back in. Your arms will swim and your head must turn to inhale at the appropriate time. But you cannot inhale until you exhale at least 20% of your air supply. When you cannot breathe in you have to stop swimming. This is a bad timing problem and why the next step is necessary.

6. EXHALE BIG BUBBLES OVER YOUR CHEEKS

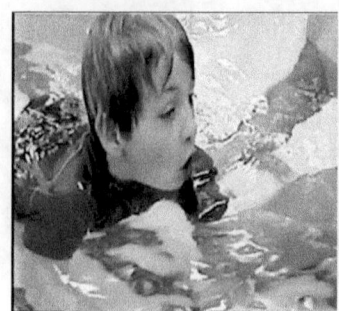 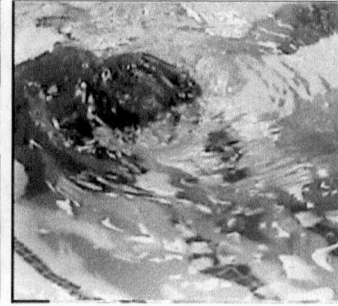 

To discriminate between blowing out slower smaller bubbles felt over your cheeks, open your mouth wider and slowly force out a large bubble or two to feel it go around and over your cheeks. Note how this feels entirely different than the small bubbles you just felt. When you practice this skill be sure your forehead is looking down at the bottom or you will blow bubbles up your nose.

By being relaxed and opening your mouth wider, you can expel at least 20% of your air in a much shorter period of time. Like walking in the park you must continually replace a portion of your air supply or you will build up an oxygen debt and have to stop walking or swimming as the case may be.

To regain your level body position after you have taken a breath, you have to put your forehead and face back down in the water looking at the bottom, and start to exhale immediately. This gives you more time to expel enough air to inhale new air when your head turns and clears the water surface as you roll your head and body up to breathe with every right arm stroke. You cannot wait to exhale when you start to turn your head; it's too late to get out enough air to breathe any amount back in and keep your body position level.

7. FACE UNDER THE SHOWER

By now you have plenty of experience rinsing soap out of your hair in the shower. Yet, you managed to inhale despite the cascade of water flowing around your face. Learning to swim with your breathing is no different. You get used to having your face in the water exhaling large bubbles, and as you rotate your face up to breathe you inhale a small breath. You don't suck in your air any harder than you would in the shower.

8. CHILD GUIDANCE - POUR RINSE WATER OVER YOUR CHILD'S HEAD

Prior to soaping your child's head up, take a plastic container and scoop clean water up from the tub to gently pour over his head a few times when he is sitting or on his stomach. Do this while your child is still very young and make it a fun activity.

Do not be alarmed if your child starts to cry or scream and does not like what you do. Simply continue to do this until he gets used to it. Make this as normal as getting in the tub. Infants are like golden retrievers, and easily sense your concerns. As the parent, you must not show any fear, but create the idea that this is a regular activity.

Step 2 Dressing mirror progressive sequence

9. TORPEDO STEP

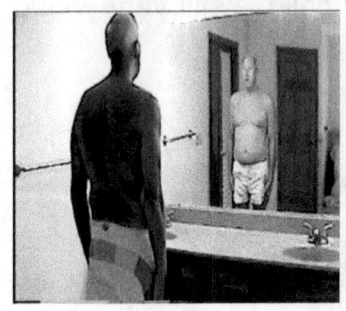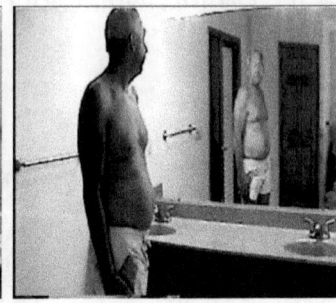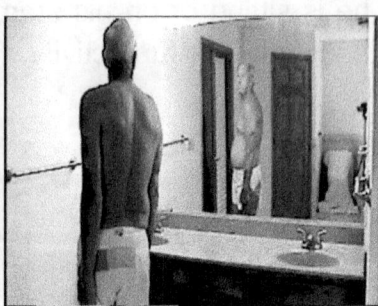

Look directly at your eyes in a dressing mirror. If your eyes in the mirror start to move, it's not the mirror. Stand up straight with your feet planted firmly on the floor hip width apart. Imagine a rod fixed from your head to your toes about which you are going to roll your upper body around like a spindle while keeping your feet fixed. This step looks like a torpedo that can roll, but do not move your head or body from side to side or up and down out of the rod alignment.

This action will be most like when you actually swim on top of the water in a floating position. Now you have the opportunity out of the water to practice and build a motor pattern with specific skills steps and cues, and transfer these same identical elements to the shallow end of the pool when you are ready. By practicing at home you can develop these basic fundamentals to build your confidence, and learn to apply them easily when you get to a shallow pool.

Focus on keeping your eyes and head steady in the mirror so your brain will not process extra information. Roll each shoulder forward and backward so that one is in front of the other, and then reverse it to twist your upper body. Keep your head steady. There is no bobbing or weaving rolling about that imaginary rod to teach you how to stay on plane. Only your shoulders and upper torso do the twisting and rolling about your hips. Keep your feet in place so your brain can focus on the skill and not process extra information.

10. PROPELLER STEP

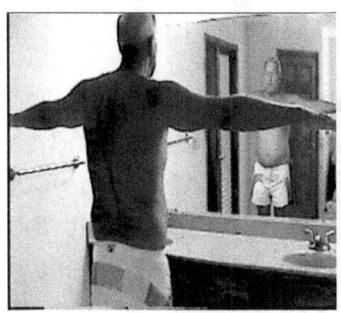 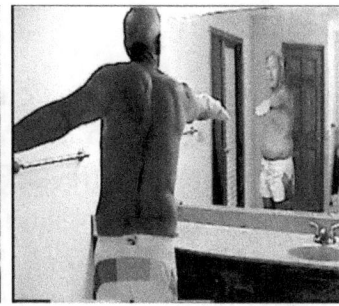 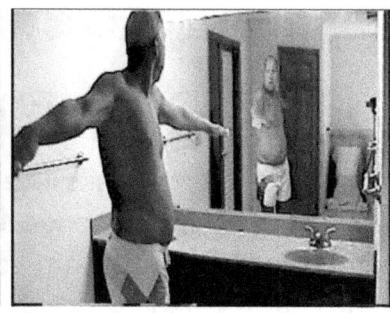

Lift your arms up straight from your sides so that they are completely level with your shoulders and opposite from one another. As you did in your torpedo step, I want you to rotate and place one shoulder and arm extended from that shoulder in front of the other with the other trailing directly opposite behind you. When you look in the mirror you can see that your trailing arm and shoulder are completely opposite from your forward arm and shoulder.

Focus on keeping your head steady and not allow your arm to catch up without the complete shoulder roll. You gain valuable feedback by making sure that your arms remain level with the tops of your shoulders. Practice slowly rotating each <u>arm and shoulder</u> opposite to one another back and forth several times.

11. SEESAW STEP

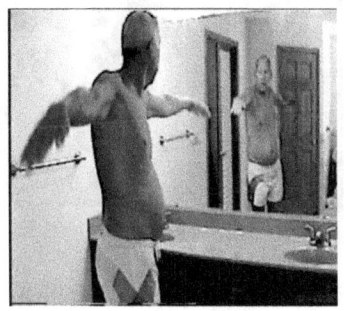  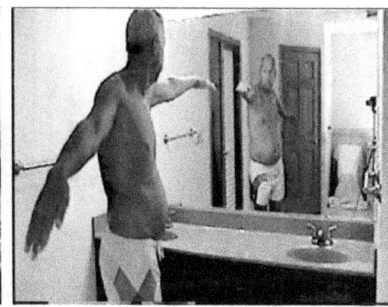

Your neck becomes the fulcrum and with your arms extended as you did in the propeller step, hold your lead arm and shoulder forward and rotate downward. At the same time as your lead arm and shoulder goes downward, like in a seesaw, your trailing shoulder, arm and hand must go upward to condition the feeling of this opposing motion. When the lead arm goes down, the trailing arm must lift up like a seesaw. This is what swimming will be like while floating. Keep your feet, head, and eyes fixed to focus all your attention on learning this step.

12. WINDMILL (FERRIS WHEEL) STEP

Start to imagine pulling yourself forward with your lead arm. Your trailing arm must start to lift up and come around to begin the next stroke and so on. This pattern looks like a windmill or carnival Ferris wheel. Keep your hands and arms opposite one another rotating your torso about the imaginary rod. Focus on your eyes in the mirror to keep your head steady. This gross motor action does not resemble good technique, but is necessary to gain a better feel for what you will transfer to floating in the pool.

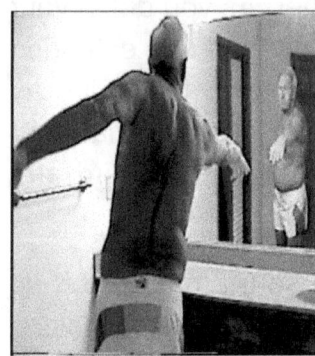

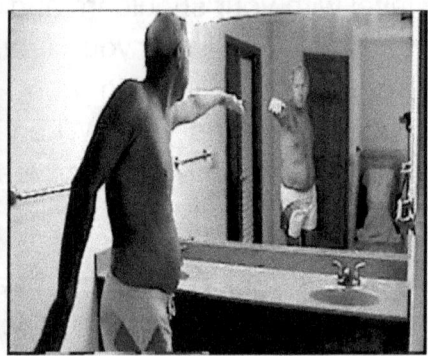

13. PIVOT STEP

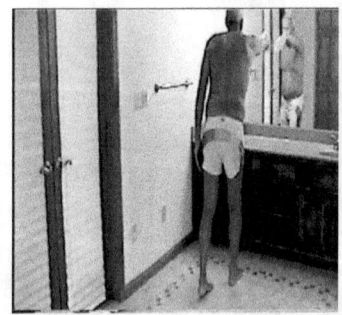
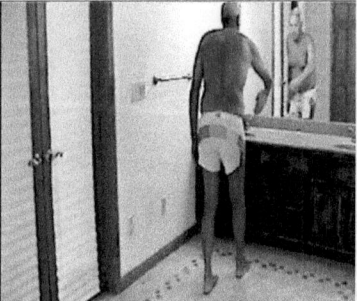
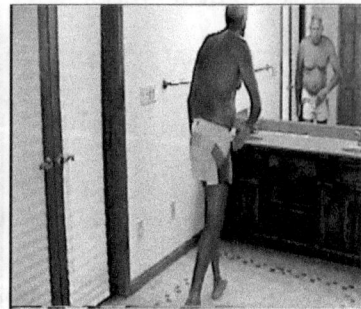

Like a basketball pivot step use your non-dominant foot (usually your left foot if you are right-handed). Fix that foot to the floor and step forward onto your right foot. You will learn to breathe on your dominant and stronger right arm. As you step forward onto your right foot, look into the mirror to see how you lift up your shoulder, arm and hand to extend your reach forward from your shoulder into the "hole." The "hole" is where both hands are together with fully extended arms to start your catch in the face float position you just performed in previous mattress steps. This action helps you increase your distance per stroke and be more efficient.

That imaginary rod going through your head down between your legs creates a midline plane you can observe in the mirror. Use your lead hand to rotate below your elbow, and follow that imaginary midline downward and backward. Pretend you are pulling and pushing yourself forward through the water while floating streamlined and level. At the same time roll and pivot step back to let your hand clear your hips and keep your hand following that imaginary midline.

As you roll your hips back to clear for your hand, be sure to follow through to push yourself forward like doing a push up before exiting your hand and arm out of the water. Emphasize rolling your shoulder back to make your forearm and hand exit with your palm flat. This makes it easier for your shoulder joint to recover your arms while swimming to avoid injury.

Note: If you are a competitive swimmer with shoulder joint problems, this is how to correct the mechanics that cause some of it.

14. SUMMARY REVIEW

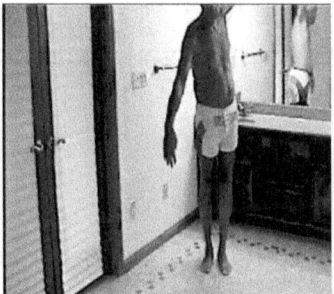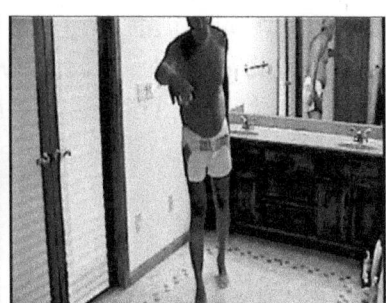

You have now mastered five key home steps in front of your dressing mirror to transfer the same identical elements to the shallow end of the pool. The only difference will be to hold your breath and learn to float in the shallow end first before applying these steps. Or, if you prefer, you can repeat these exact same steps standing in the shallow end of the pool, and fixing your eyes on a wall or deck object.

It's important to master each of these specific steps to build your confidence and physical pattern to make them familiar skills. This becomes task familiarity. The more familiar you are with a task, the more confident and secure you will be. All these are learnable skills you can teach yourself and others.

15. CHILD GUIDANCE- KEEP THEIR HEAD STEADY AND BODY STANDING UP STRAIGHT WITH EYE CONTACT; INTRODUCE NEUTRAL POSITION

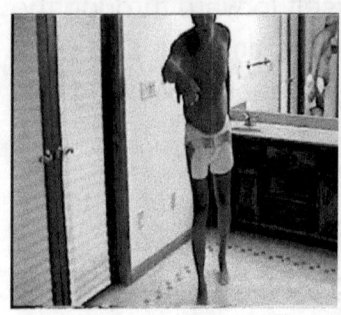 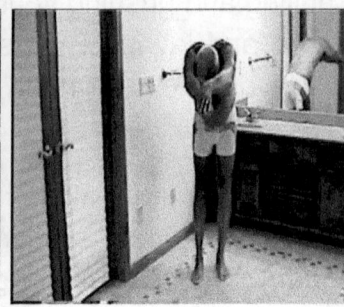 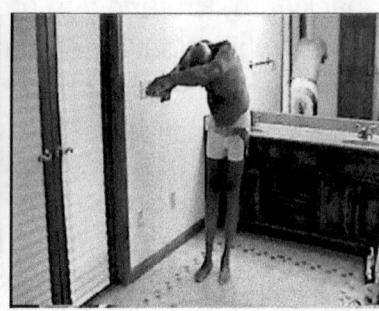

When you teach your child as a parent or grandparent insist that they do not fidget and keep their feet in place and focus their eyes in the mirror or on an object at the pool to keep their head steady. They need to learn how to rotate their body about that imaginary rod to be efficient. In order to learn these skills rapidly, the body must maintain its position to be efficient. If your body is moving all over the place, your brain must process all of that extra sensory information. This will not help you focus on a specific body part to learn that skill. Then all of their motor patterns can be observed, focused, and felt in the muscles correctly to behaviorally condition the routine.

Step 3 Mattress progressive sequence

16. NEUTRAL POSITION

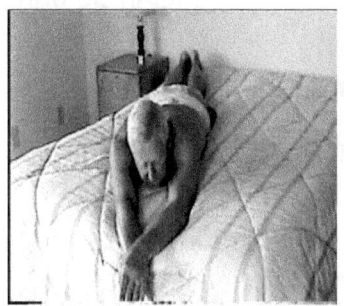  

The mattress on your bed is a perfect place for you to stretch out your body or your child's body and learn what it feels like to be perfectly level. To be streamlined keep your upper arms pinned against your ears and legs together while lying on your stomach with your forehead resting on the mattress. Point your toes slightly so that your ankles rest completely flat on the mattress, and put one hand on top of the other.

This helps you acquire spatial awareness, a key teaching method I use. Then when you float in the pool holding your breath, you'll put your face down to keep your legs and feet on the surface. This is a learnable skill, and you can do it. Then when you get to a pool and do your floating steps, you can easily transfer this skill to do a push off and glide keeping your body perfectly level on top of the water in that face float position also known as your neutral position.

17. CHILD GUIDANCE- ANKLE BOUNCE AND FISHING ROD FLIP

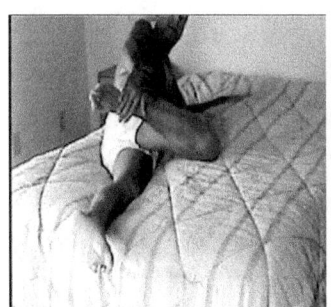 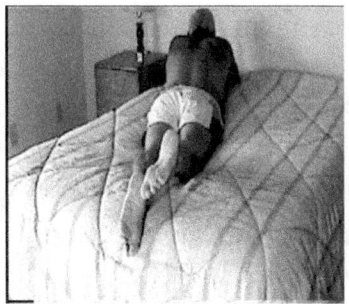 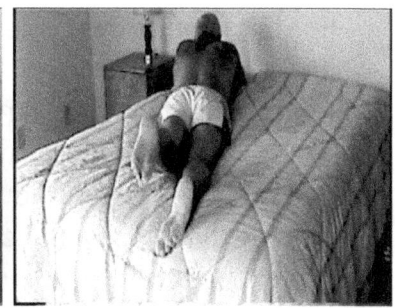

Focus on the cue "tops of your ankles" that will beat and bounce on the mattress. Get a 1-2-1-2 rhythm count. Your ankles will not separate much if you imagine you are kicking both feet inside of a 5 gallon bucket. If you focus on the wrong cue to bend your knees, your ankles will lift up too high off the mattress to create drag resistance outside of the midline plane when swimming.

In the water your kick will not provide nearly as much propulsion as your arms. If you overly focus on your kick you will spend lots of energy when you should focus on your arms to provide you with more propulsion.

One way to help your child learn is to place two fingers above and below his knee with your thumb directly behind his calf. If he tries to lift the lower leg up too high from the knee, your thumb will provide a stop like you would use on a fishing rod and reel. You can also use your thumb to alternately press his calf back down to bounce the tops of his ankles on the mattress to teach the proper rhythm and counting 1-2-1-2..., etc.

18. SIDE ROLL KICKING WITH ONE ARM EXTENDED - PRACTICE ON EACH SIDE

Your brain has a built in compass and level to keep your body in balance. Put your body into this position to see and feel what the arm pattern will be like pulling when swimming. Practice on both sides.

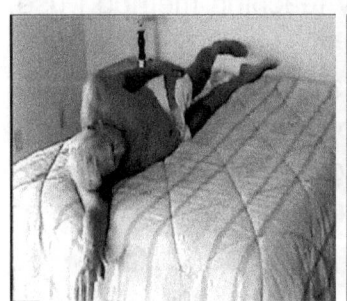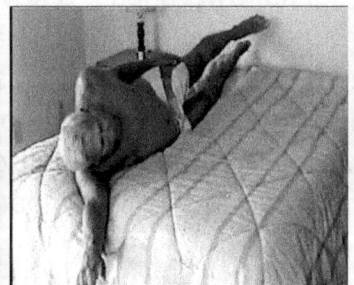

For this step extend one arm on the bottom directly forward, rest on your side, and do the same kick you did lying flat. Learn how your body rolls when you're actually swimming so that your feet and legs will also stay somewhat together kicking on each side and stroking, too. Do not over kick, but allow your feet and lower legs to separate only 6-8" off the imaginary midline to reduce resistance and be more efficient. When swimming, your feet may separate 12-18 inches.

19. KICKING ON YOUR SIDE ONE ARM STROKING - PRACTICE ON EACH SIDE

 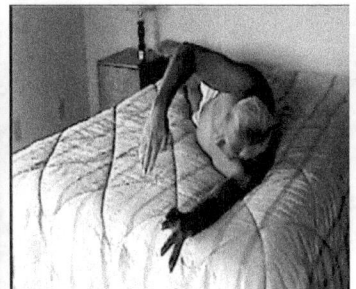 

Repeat the previous step and use your top arm to pretend you are swimming to coordinate with your kick. Do an elliptical stroke with your free hand and bent forearm while resting on your non-breathing arm side initially. Once you master that skill roll onto your breathing side arm, continue to kick moderately, and practice stroking with your other arm. You get the sensation of being level on each side while stroking and maintaining a moderate kick at the same time. This is designed to transfer the same identical elements from home to the shallow end of the pool.

20. RHYTHM KICKING ANKLES OFF THE MATTRESS

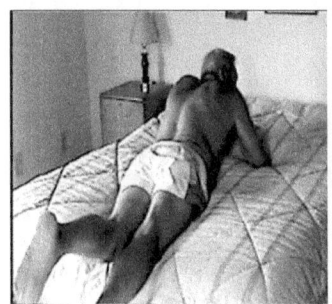 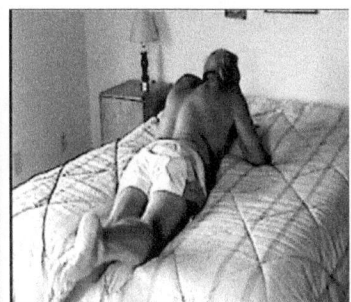 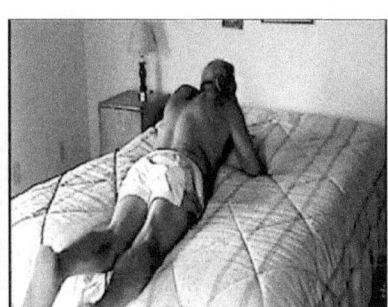

Extend your lower legs off the mattress so you will not feel the tops of your ankles beat down on the mattress. Keep your ankles and legs together so they do not overly separate and go outside of the midline to create resistance. Keep a moderate natural rhythm. This will make your transition to the water much easier.

21. CHILD GUIDANCE- FISHING ROD FLIP

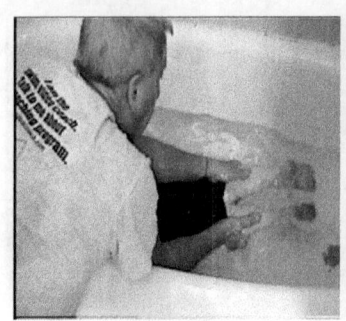 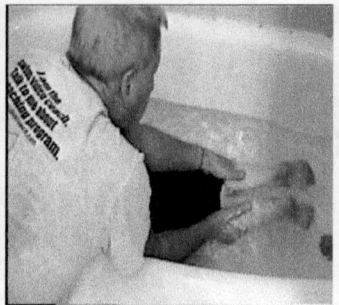 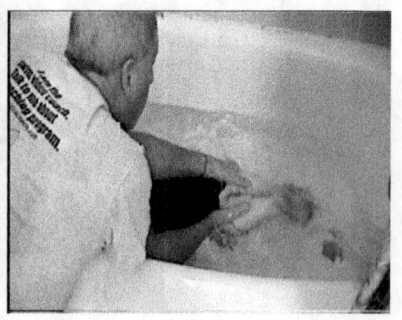

For parents, place two fingers above and below your child's kneecap, and use your thumb as a brake to prevent his lower leg from lifting up too far out of the water or off the mattress. You can also press your thumb into the lower leg as if you were casting with your fishing rod to initiate the rhythm, and count out loud for them to hear 1-2-1-2 for a moderate kick. Do not allow large splashing kicks. You can cast the lower leg with your two fingers, and quickly press the lower leg back down with your thumb to create the moderate rhythm.

Step 4 Bath tub progressive sequence

22. ON STOMACH FACE IN CUPPED HANDS

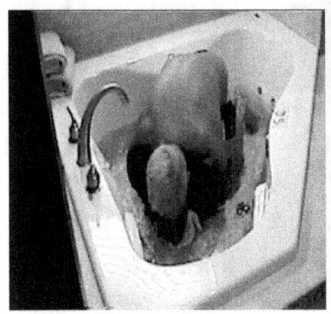 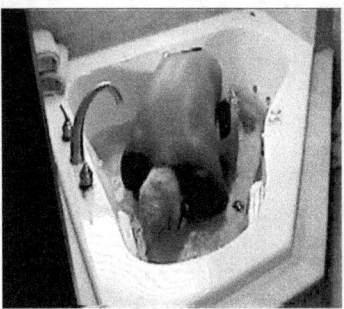 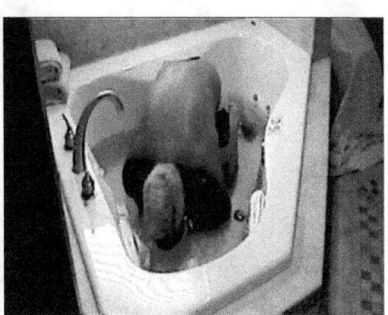

Your bathtub is a perfect place to practice. You may have to bend your legs to be able to get your torso in the water if you're very tall, and you can place your face in your hands to practice getting used to having your nose in the water. Now you can repeat the kitchen sink steps.

I want to caution you not to overfill your bathtub. When you lie in the tub your torso will displace that much more water that can cascade over the side of your tub and ruin your flooring.

23. REPEAT BLOWING BIG BUBBLES

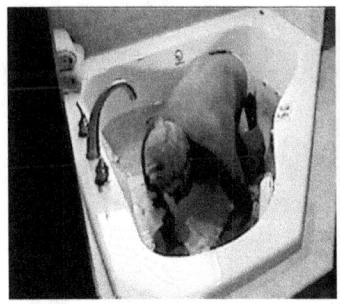 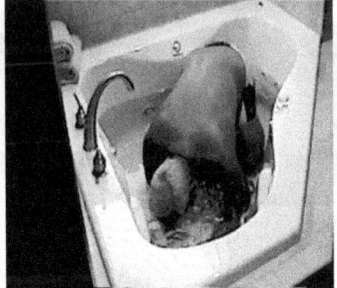 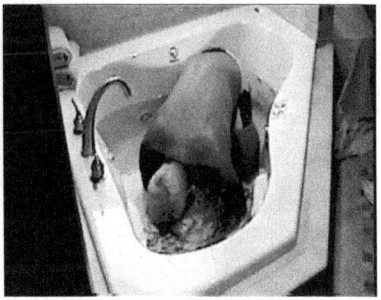

With your face in your cupped hands you can either pinch your nose or get used to going without pinching your nose, and start to blow out big bubbles as you did before in the kitchen sink. Focus on opening your mouth a little wider. Then slowly exhale a large quantity of air to feel larger bubbles form out of your mouth and go up and over your cheeks. Feel the difference between small and large bubbles.

24. ON YOUR BACK LET YOUR ARMS FLOAT UP BY YOUR SIDES

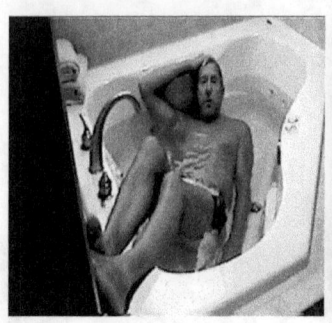 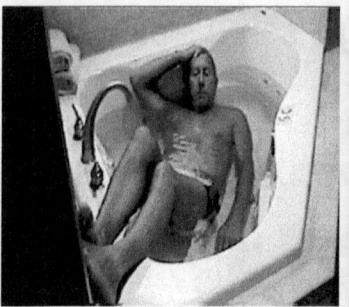 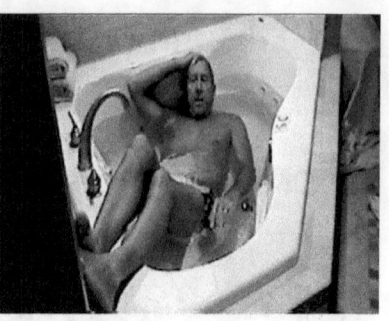

This may not be a problem for your child, but you may have to bend your knees to lift up your legs in order to fit your torso flat in the tub. Hold your arms at your sides. Then totally relax both arms to let them float freely to the surface. Feel how your body parts can float.

By learning that your parts float, you realize that you are part of the problem by interfering and being stiff in your musculature. You also teach yourself mind control over your body parts to send a correct message to your muscles to relax or to increase power. Either way this involves controlling your body parts with your mind, and is an important step to master.

25. ON YOUR BACK - DEEP INHALE AND EXHALE

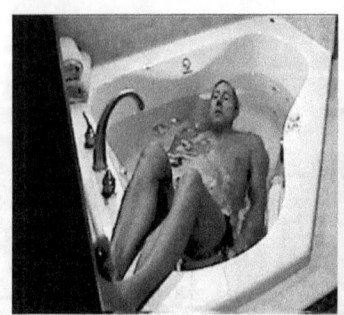 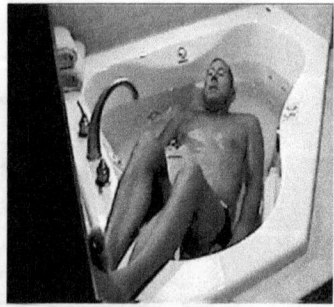 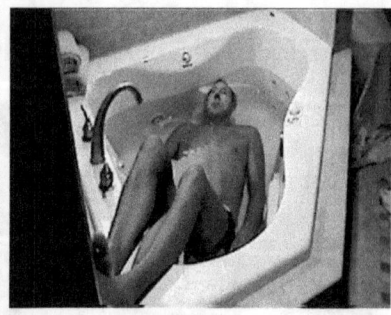

With your torso lying flat on the tub floor, inhale slowly, and feel your chest rise. Then slowly exhale to feel your chest start to fall. Repeat this several times to realize that if you inflate your lungs you will be floating. Then when you go to the pool, stand on the bottom and lower your torso up to your shoulders or lie on one of the steps. You can repeat the same identical element floating in your tub to develop your confidence.

26. MODERATE KICK ON YOUR STOMACH

This step will be easier for your child to perform in the tub than you. Repeat the same moderate rhythm kick that you did bouncing your ankles off the mattress. For children, use the shower curtain so that they don't splash water out of the tub. Children can get very vigorous and overly kick their ankles. Remind him to do only a moderate kick keeping his ankles and legs closer together as if he were kicking inside of a 5 gallon bucket.

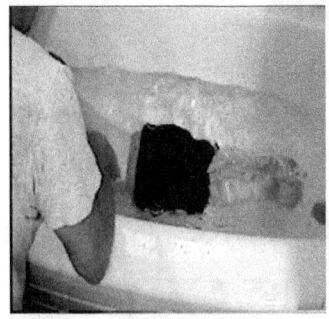 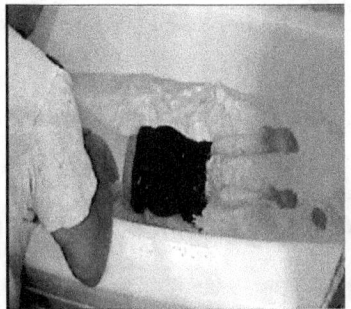 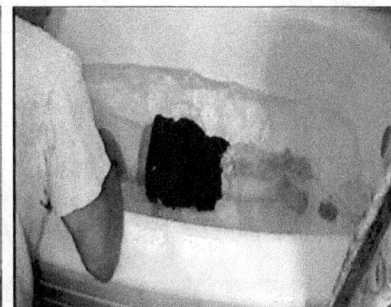

Condition a moderate kick to feel the rhythm and be able to keep your feet on the surface without dragging your legs down to be inefficient. Your mind has to condition what your body parts do to get spatial awareness, and know where each body part is at any given moment.

27. MODERATE KICK ON YOUR BACK

  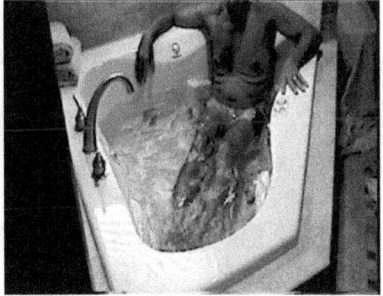

Adults can sit in the tub and hopefully your legs are not longer than your tub to observe your kick. You can see and feel what you are doing at the same time to know that your feet are kicking as if they were in a 5 gallon bucket and not overly separate. Rather than point your toes to plantar flex your ankle, let your ankles relax so that the water pressure turns your feet into flippers. Only your toes will chip the water surface.

28. ON YOUR SIDE ONE-ARMED WINDMILL - PRACTICE ON EACH SIDE

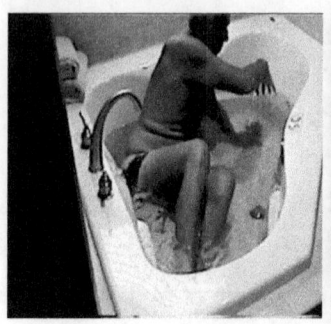  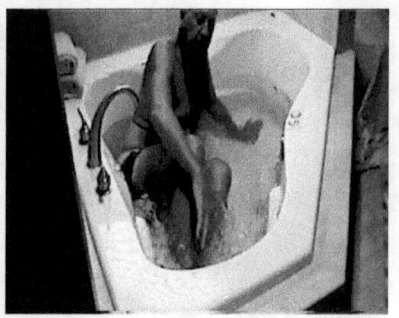

Repeat the mattress step lying on one side, but bend your knees up to fit in the tub. Try to stroke one hand in the water to feel some water pressure.

29. ON YOUR SIDE ONE-ARM WINDMILL WITH MODERATE KICK

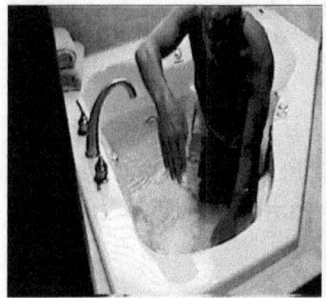  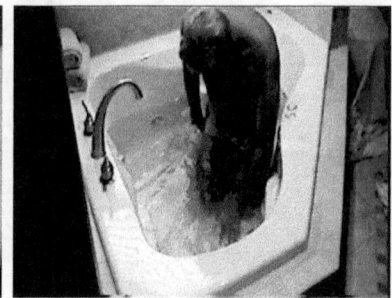

Do the previous step one-arm windmill and moderately alternate your ankles from side to side in a moderate kick.

This is a great way for small children to learn the rhythm of their kick along with stroking their arm. Be sure to practice on both sides.

30. ON YOUR SIDE ONE-ARMED WINDMILL WITH BREATHING TO BLOW BIG BUBBLES

 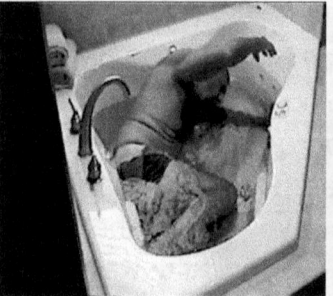 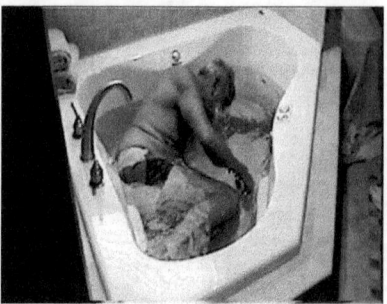

Where possible try to roll your body and face into the water, and blow large bubbles as you repeat the previous step. This is ideal for conditioning breathing sequences for young children without having to be in the swimming pool. Then when you go to the pool, you can make the transition much more easily. Again, you will place your hand in the water to feel some kind of water pressure on your hand and forearm, but not stroke so hard that you splash water out of the tub.

31. **CHILD GUIDANCE - FISHING ROD FLIP FOR THE KICK; TWO FINGERS HOLD THE WRIST OF THE STROKING ARM (DO SAME LYING IN THE TUB AS ON POOL SIDE)**

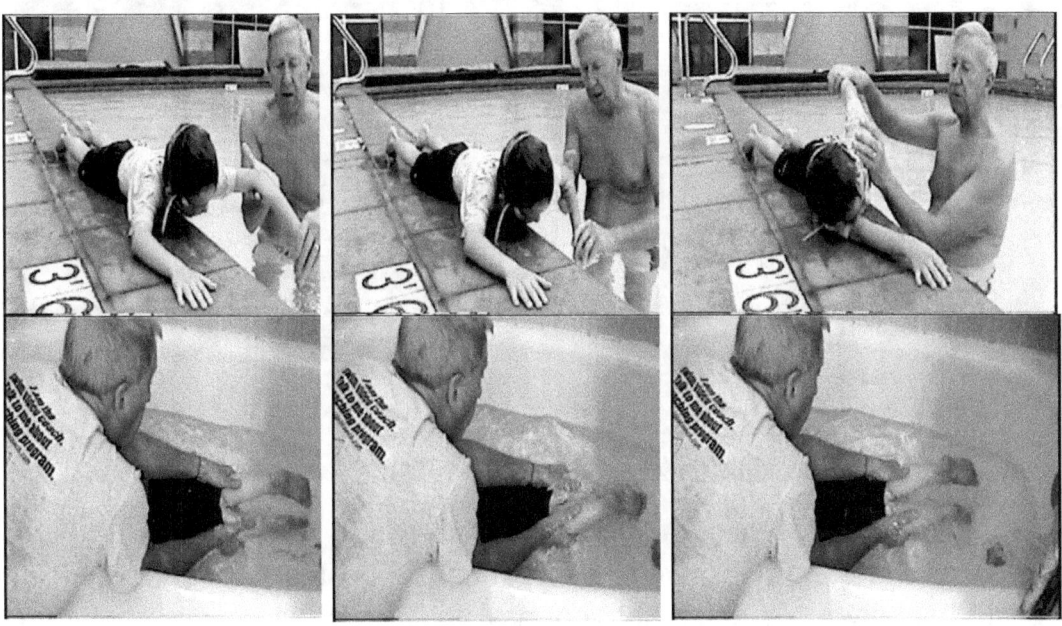

Hold your child's wrists between your index and middle fingers, and thumb to guide him through the arm pull pattern. Make sure that he completes each stroke and lifts his shoulder, arm, and hand up out of the water or the tub. You can also practice the fishing rod flip in the tub as you did on the mattress, and monitor these initial patterns to master them.

To focus on lifting the hand and arm up out of the water, ask him to reach up to touch the ceiling or grab a cloud out of the sky.

Step 5   Observe pool health and safety signs and depth markings

32   POSTED RULES AND HEALTH REGULATIONS

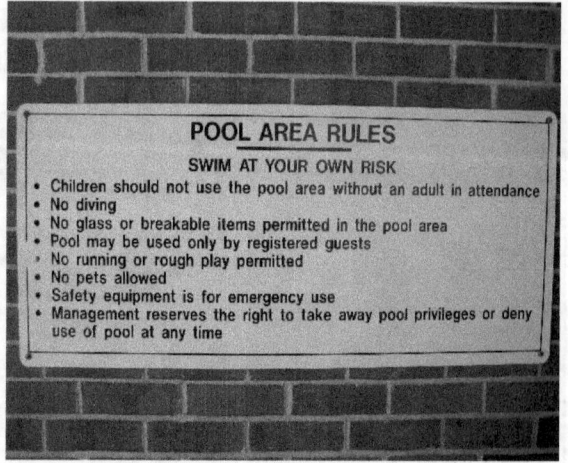

Local and state health regulations must be posted in every swimming pool. These typically state that you may not swim in the public pool if you have a communicable disease or open sores. Bandages and dressings will come off in the water. Parents are also cautioned that their infants need to wear plastic retaining pants over their diapers, and immediately remove their children from the water if they have a bowel movement.

All pools are periodically tested each day for water clarity and chemical content to keep the chemicals that disinfect the pool in balance to acceptable parts per million bacteria level. Lifeguards must be trained and certified to do their job. However, it is always your personal responsibility to monitor your children and your own activities in the water.

The lifeguards are not your kid-sitter. You must know your child's abilities and skills for every environment.

Typical rules are that you may not take glass containers or food on the deck. You should not be allowed to chew gum and swim, and you must be able to pass a distance test to swim in the deep end and go off the diving boards. Diving boards have their own set of rules, more or less imposed by insurance companies that track accidents. This is why you don't see many 3 meter diving boards.

Diving board rules include one on a board at a time, waiting for the diver to clear out from under the board, and no double bouncing or inward, back, and reverse dives.

Under crowded conditions you may not be allowed to use inner tubes, rafts, balls, or other such objects that restrict the lifeguard's clear view of the occupants. Local rules may also limit pool capacity on hot days and close the pool on cold days if the occupancy drops below a certain number.

And don't be upset if asked to clear the pool with the sound of thunder. Cloud to ground lightning has been seen landing a half mile from the cloud. Standing under the roof overhang of the locker room is not good. Go inside out of danger, and if you are on the water, boating, get to shore and cover in a building.

33   SAFETY WARNING SIGNS

Typical warning signs are posted on the fence, wall, or deck to indicate no diving, running, glass containers, food, smoking, etc. You will also see the deep end separated by a rope with several floats on it.

34 DEPTH MARKINGS

By state law public pools are required to paint on the deck or post on the wall the depth of the pool at that mark. An indoor pool showed the pool bottom contour on a line directly on the wall so that you could walk on that side of the pool and know exactly how deep it was to jump in at that point.

Know the pool depth and your height to your mouth and not your head to stand up and breathe. Even if you stand on your tippy toes, your mouth may not clear. Your bobbing skills are necessary to bounce off the pool bottom to get back to shallow water. The rule of thumb is don't venture into water over your chest deep until you know how to swim across the pool.

35 NOTIFY LIFEGUARDS

When you transfer your steps from home into the pool, it's wise to do this at a time when the pool is least crowded. This will provide less distraction and help you to focus on each specific step you need to practice. At some point you will want to practice swimming across a corner of the deep end only after you can swim across the shallow end without stopping.

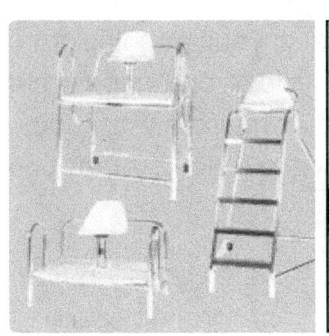  

When you are ready to swim across a corner of the deep end you must notify the lifeguards what you want to do, and choose a time when the pool is not busy. You are not allowed to swim in the diving well unless you are going off the boards. When the pool is not crowded, the lifeguard may allow you to swim across a corner to practice. This will also give them notice to keep an eye on you.

Some lifeguards may actually be on a swim team and be able to give you some feedback about how you are performing. Most likely they will encourage you to take lessons from them. They may or may not be as good an instructor as you think. You would do well to give this book and all of its steps ample time to show you that you can teach yourself very well. At the very least, you will be able to master all of the basic fundamental skills to make your private lesson more valuable for the money.

36 GOGGLES, NOSE CLIPS, EARPLUGS

 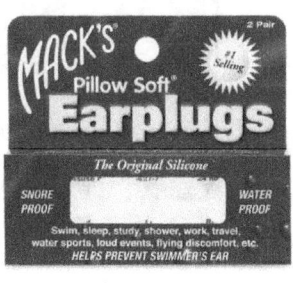

The greatest aid you can buy is a good pair of goggles for $12-$18. Get silicone seals and an adjustable separated head strap at the crown of your head to keep them from slipping down on top of your ears. This will allow you to keep your eyes open underwater when floating or swimming to see your stroke mechanics and make corrections. To keep your goggles from fogging up, put a thin layer of your saliva on the inside lens and rinse it out before you apply them. You can buy goggles online at major swim shops. What I recommend are the Speedo hydro-specs or Vanquisher 2.0 that you can buy from www.Kiefer.com or www.AllAmericanSwim.com.

I don't like nose clips except to learn backstroke. If water goes up your nose you need to keep your mouth open, and lower your forehead so that when you blow bubbles they will not shoot up your nose.

Nose clips prevent you from exhaling a portion of your air through your nose to help expel the bad air in order to inhale and replace your air supply as you swim. If you keep your mouth open in the water, you will form a good air lock in your nose to prevent water from going up and tickling the hairs in your nose.

Earplugs may be another answer if you continually have ear infections. I recommend that after you swim, shake the water out of your ear and put a small quantity of toilet paper on your little finger to dry your outer ear canal. This will help to prevent fungus infections in your ear canal. If you must wear earplugs get the moldable wax kind to fit in your ear canal better.

37 ENTERING AND EXITING THE POOL

Plan to enter the pool using the ladder or steps or ease in from the side when you know the depth markings and your height. Use the ladders to reduce the risk of slipping your grip on the side and falling with your face on the deck especially if you are older and lack the upper arm strength. Some pools provide a chairlift that is powered by a hand crank or water pressure from a hose.

Step 6 Transfer home skills to the shallow end of a pool or lake

Waist deep for the learner and not the parent is appropriate. Then work next to the wall for added security. Use the ladder or steps. The steps work great to get the right depth and practice the same steps you learned at home.

This may seem too repetitious, but the motor patterns are still being formed adding the associations from the pool. As beginners become more familiar with simple tasks, they build their confidence and become less apprehensive to learn each new step.

38 RHYTHMICAL KICKING 1-2-1-2 SITTING ON THE EDGE WITH YOUR FEET IN THE WATER

Sit on the pool edge and extend your feet over the water. Relax your ankles but keep them close together. As you chip the water and lift your ankle, the water pressure will flex your feet like flippers. Count out loud 1-2-1-2 to get your rhythm. Visualize what you are feeling keeping your ankles and legs together as if you were kicking inside of a 5 gallon bucket. Note that as you lift your foot up the water pressure will force your toes down to give you the relaxed ankle and flipper action you want once you get in the water, start to float, and kick moderately on your stomach.

39 BUCKET KICK - JUST THE ANKLES; FEET RELAXED; FEEL WATER PRESSURE FLIPPER YOUR FEET

Imagine a 5 gallon bucket that is 1 foot in diameter. Pretend your feet are kicking inside of that bucket and will not allow you to separate your ankles that much. Once you visualize sitting on the deck and doing that, you can then perform that skill by feel when you're floating on your stomach and can't see your kick. With your ankles relaxed you will also be able to feel the natural rhythm that the water creates with your ankle. Be sure to focus on the alternating rhythm.

When you practice a visual and kinesthetic feeling cue together this is called "paired-associate" conditioning to aid learning.

40 REPEAT ALL THE DRESSING MIRROR STEPS EYES STAY FIXED ON AN OBJECT ON THE DECK OR POOL WALL

Earlier I wrote about transferring the same identical elements you learned at home to use in the pool. First practice them on the deck, and then standing in the shallow end of the pool. Repeat every step sequence that you did at home. Locate an object on the deck and keep your feet in place. Focus your eyes on that object. Your head will not move but your body will do all the steps to rotate your torso and hips keeping your feet in place.

By groups of 3 – Torpedo, Propeller, See Saw, Windmill, Pivot

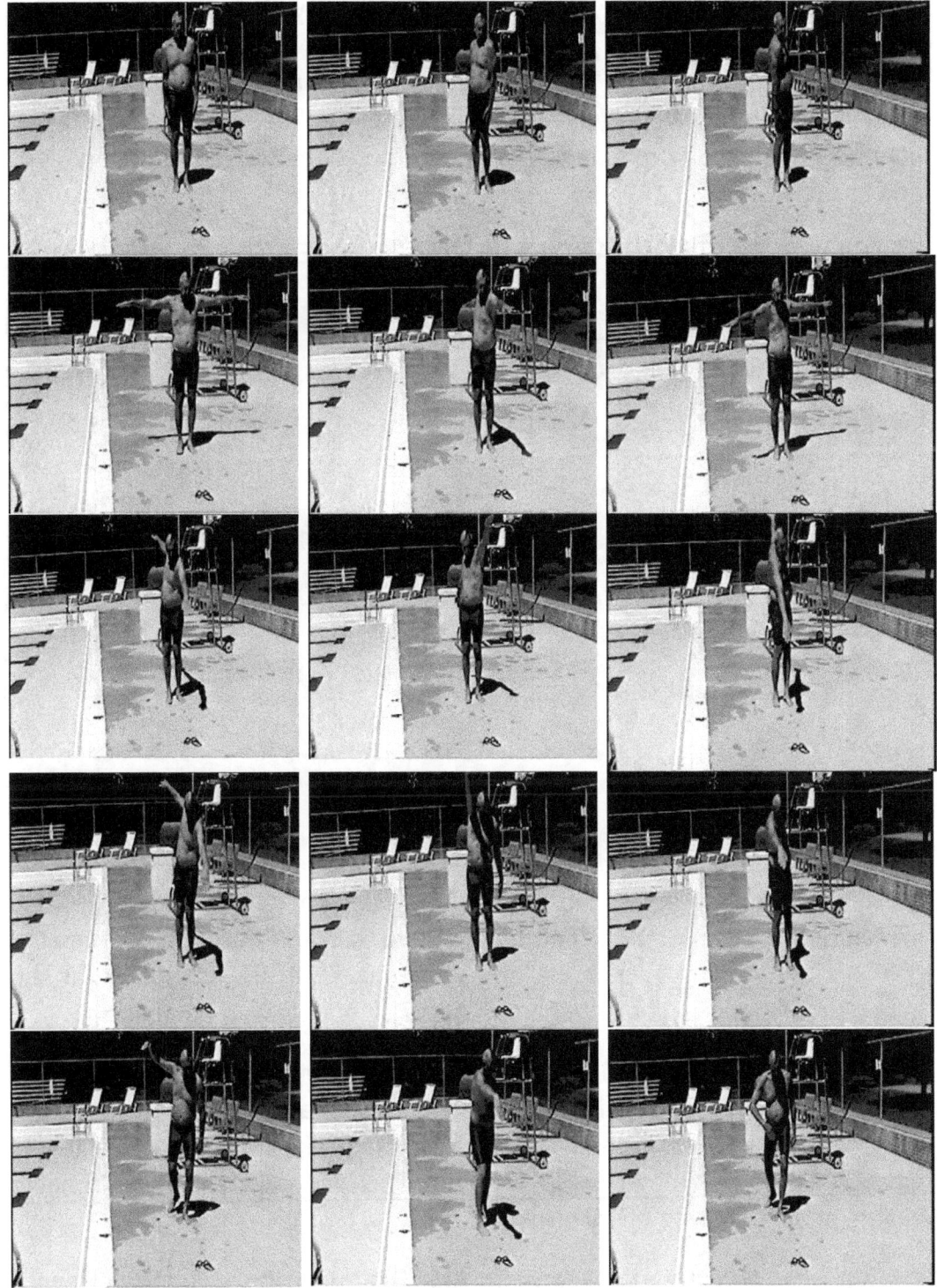

In sequence order, repeat all the steps you did in front of the dressing mirror starting with the torpedo, propeller, seesaw, windmill, and then the pivot step. Do each as accurately as you did at home in order to master them on the pool deck as well. All of this will help you to master swimming efficiently much faster. Be patient. Take it one step at a time. Each of these early steps provides the fundamental foundation to becoming a very efficient swimmer. When you swim, you'll need to keep your balance when your body is rolling from side to side to alternately move your arms and legs and breathe.

41 DEMONSTRATE 25 YARD FREESTYLE TO GET THE GENERAL IDEA

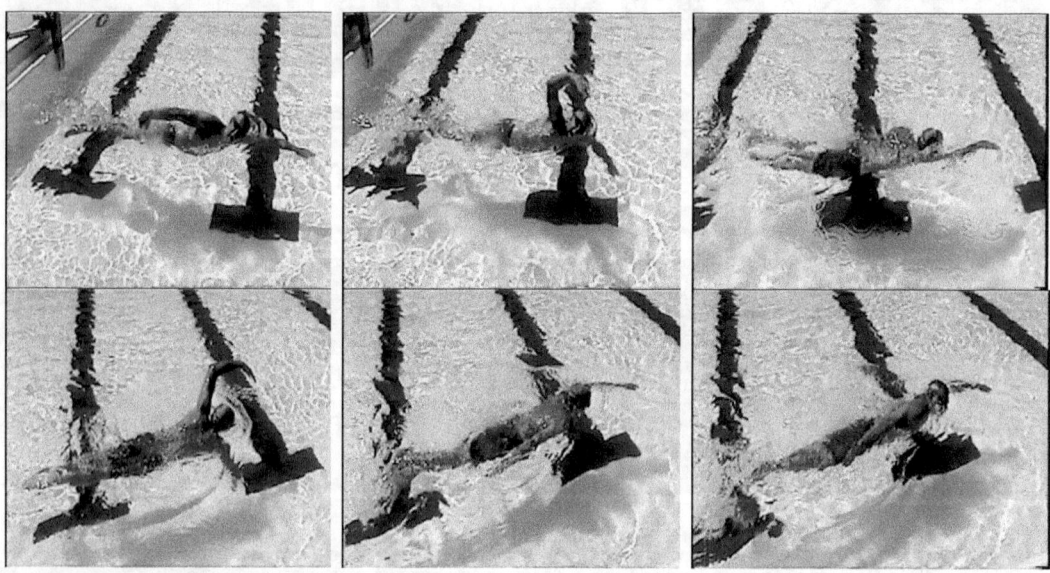

From the thumbnail pictures you can see a general idea of the coordination of the arms, legs, and body position to swim freestyle also known as front crawl. Note that my body starts out in the face float neutral position, and begins to pull one arm alternating with the other arm. I can take a breath, and replenish a portion of my air supply with each stroke.

In the face float position while holding your breath, start a moderate kick just to keep your legs and feet in the float position and not create excessive drag or resistance, and then add your arms. Take longer strokes to get more distance per stroke while floating. This will give you more time to exhale and inhale with every stroke.

It is always better to take a few good strokes than a lot of fast poor ones.

42 NEXT TO THE WALL OR STEPS PUT YOUR FACE UNDERWATER - IN CUPPED HANDS

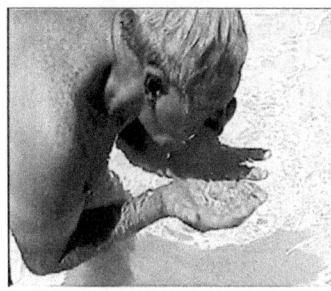 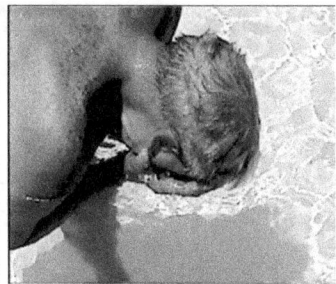 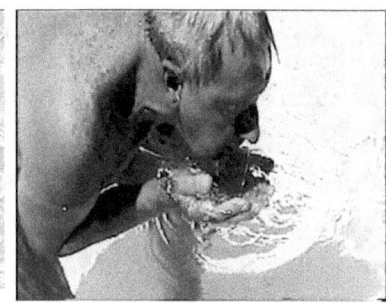

Standing next to the wall or steps put your face in the water. You can lower one hand as you did in the kitchen sink to put your face in that cupped hand and pinch your nose with the other hand, or hold on to the wall. Try not to pinch your nose, but open your mouth wider to relax. Use your mind to control any fears and replace negative images of failure with positive images of success.

To swim efficiently you need to put your face and head in the water looking directly at the pool bottom so that your body will float level. Otherwise, if you raise your head out of water your hips will go down to create excessive amounts of drag and be inefficient. This uses up your air supply quickly and causes you to get into trouble. Now is the time to practice and master this step before you proceed to the next step and so on.

43 FINGER IN YOUR MOUTH

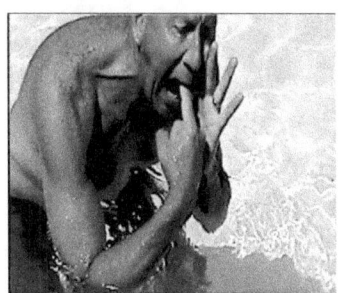  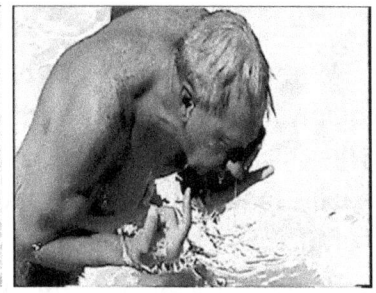

As I had you do in the kitchen sink, you will transfer the same identical element of opening your mouth to twirl around your index finger to demonstrate to your brain that you will not inhale water and drown. Master this step to recognize that you form an airlock with your mouth and nose. The water will not automatically rush in to fill your lungs; you are not going to inhale water. Neither will the air come out unless you force it out of your lungs more readily with your mouth open to exhale large bubbles.

44 SLOWLY EXHALE BIG BUBBLES OVER YOUR CHEEKS

As you did in your kitchen sink, now you will do this standing in shallow water next to the wall for security. Open your mouth wide enough to force out large bubbles that you can feel moving over your cheeks. This is a mind control step that you must master to feel relaxed and comfortable with your face in the water.

When you swim you need to exhale very quickly only 20% of your air supply with every stroke. You'll have plenty of air left to keep you afloat. This is made possible by keeping your mouth open to expel the air more easily than you would if you tried to blow out a candle and had your lips pursed. To practice you can put one hand on the wall and the other hand on your thigh or directly below your mouth when you go to exhale. This will help you to focus on a wider mouth blowing large bubbles.

45 HOLD THE WALL - SLOWLY BOBBING COMPLETELY UNDERWATER AND REPEAT 2-3 TIMES IN A ROW UNTIL RELAXED

To master rhythmical breathing and improve your timing while swimming you must master this bobbing action. You can easily exhale and inhale in one motion without having to stop. Focus on going all the way underwater and exhale continuously for several seconds as you are coming up. Then when your head rises out of the water, stop exhaling and start inhaling the same amount of air that you exhaled and bob back underwater.

To master this skill you are not allowed to stop and inhale twice. You must maintain a continuous rhythm like it will be when you swim with the same timing for at least 2-3 bobs.

You are transferring the same identical elements you will experience when actually swimming. You are not allowed to stop swimming in order to exhale and inhale with your head above the water. **Once you take a breath, you need to put your head back down and start to exhale immediately.** Your mouth is always open! Now bring your other arm around so that you will swim continuously and not stop to tread water or get another breath. You need to be as efficient as you would breathe taking a moderate walk in the park where you exhale 20% of your air and inhale 20% of your air as you continuously walk only you will be continuously swimming instead.

46 RHYTHM BOBBING – WORK ON BLOWING BIG BUBBLES – OPEN YOUR MOUTH WIDER

To master the previous step you want to open your mouth perhaps a little wider each time to feel larger bubbles coming out easier in one relaxed motion. When you feel relaxed and not tense, you are closer to mastering this step. The more you practice this step, the faster you'll become an efficient swimmer.

 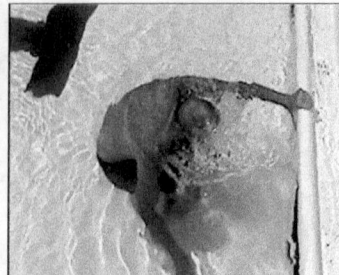 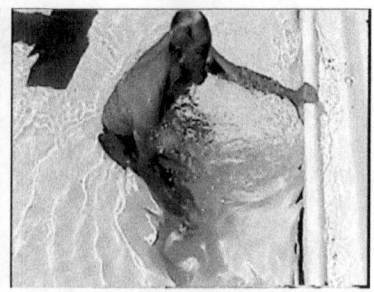
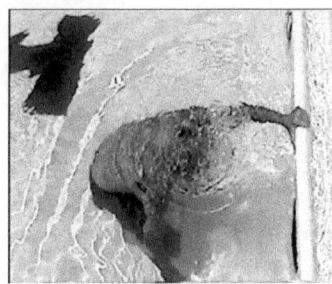  

47 CHILD GUIDANCE - EXHALE SLOWLY TO GET OUT MORE BIG BUBBLES BEFORE INHALING SLOWLY AND RELAXED IN RHYTHM

When working with small children, it's wise to give him ample time to master these steps so that he is comfortable exhaling his air and replacing it. Emphasize that he is not totally exhaling all of his air which would give him the impression that he is going to sink. Instead, emphasize he only needs to exhale a small portion of his air, and inhale that same small portion of air. This means he needs to blow out bigger bubbles and not suck the air back in, but let the air flow in naturally like he does when he is walking.

48 BREATH HOLDING 5, 10, 15, 20 SECONDS - IF YOU PINCH YOUR NOSE, THEN PRACTICE KEEPING YOUR MOUTH OPEN NOT PINCHING YOUR NOSE UNTIL RELAXED

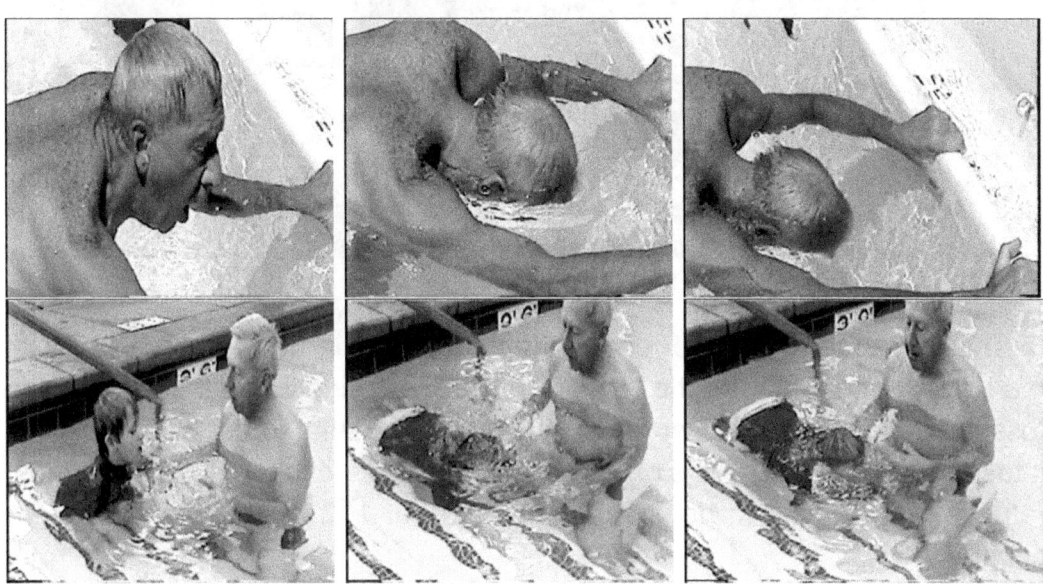

Hold the gutter or a ladder with one hand, and keep your feet planted to feel secure in the pool. Now you cannot lose your balance and panic or hit the wall when you close your eyes underwater. You must master this step with mind control. **You cannot learn to swim efficiently until you can swim by holding your breath for at least 15 to 20 seconds.** This will allow you time to feel movement in the water, and feel rewarded and motivated to master your breathing sequence to swim continuously, replacing your air supply as you swim.

This step conditions you to inhale and keep your lungs inflated to float. You must master the sensation of floating before taking strokes. This creates the correct mindset that you float first and swim second. I spend a lot of time teaching you floating skills to change your mindset from the idea that if you do not move your arms and legs you are going to sink. This is not true. But you must learn to hold your breath for 15 to 20 seconds to relax and float on top of the water.

49 OPEN YOUR EYES UNDERWATER - RELAX LOCATE AN OBJECT OR COUNT FINGERS

You can see underwater very easily with your goggles, but I suggest you get used to opening your eyes underwater without your goggles. Everything underwater will appear fuzzy at first, and you need to know what it's like just in case you are ever without your goggles.

There are many kinds of underwater objects in a pool. You can look at the lights, bottom step of the ladder, painted lane line or wall. You can also toss a coin, a rubber ring, or other object that sinks flat to not be impaled on it to look at. However, if it is on the bottom and you tossed it there, you must retrieve it. It's easier to have someone hold out 1, 2 or 3 fingers for you to count.

50 TORPEDO

  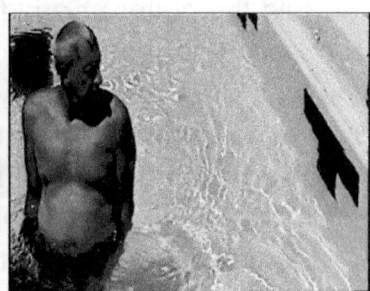

Repeat the same step that you did standing in front of the dressing mirror. Pretend that you have an imaginary rod running from your head through your body down between your legs. Be sure to keep your feet planted on the floor of the pool and your eyes fixed on an object you see on the deck or the wall so that your head will remain steady. Now learn to rotate your body about that imaginary rod. This is what it will be like when you're in a level floating position and roll your body to stroke and turn your head up to breathe. Take time to master these basic steps before you attempt to do them while floating.

51 PROPELLER

Keep your feet standing in place and raise your arms up so that your arms are level with your shoulders. Make sure that your hands and arms stay opposite from one another. Then rotate one arm and shoulder in front of the other making sure they remain opposite to one another. Make sure your arms remain level and fully extended at shoulder height to look like an airplane propeller. Fully twist your upper torso and shoulders so that each time you end up with one shoulder completely in front of the other one while you keep your head steady with your eyes fixed on that object. This is the kind of shoulder and body roll you will do swimming.

52 SEE SAW

This is the see saw or teeter-totter position where your neck is the fulcrum on your shoulders. When your lead arm starts to pull downward and backward, your trailing arm will start to lift upward and forward to remain opposite to one another the same as in front of the dressing mirror.

53 WINDMILL OR FERRIS WHEEL

Keeping your head and eyes fixed and feet planted again like you did at home, start one arm in a circular pattern like a windmill while the other arm follows in opposition to rotate up and forward as the lead arm goes downward and backward.

Your arms will be doing two separate windmills. Condition the feeling that when one arm goes down the other arm starts up. You must learn that your arm will not automatically come out of the water and swing over to get ready for another stroke unless you focus on making it do that action. Then while holding your breath floating, it will be easy to copy that same pattern with each arm.

54 RECOVERY ARM - SQUAT DOWN IN THE WATER AND MOVE ONE HAND ONLY BACK AND FORTH TO CONDITION THE RECOVERY MOVEMENT PATTERN

In waist deep water squat down so the water is over the tops of your shoulders, and put one foot in front of the other for stability. Start with your breathing arm at the end of your pull and a long stroke. Your shoulder roll up will move your forearm and hand palm flat where it exits. Keep your other hand extended forward in the neutral position.

The shortest distance between two points is a straight line. Turn your palm flat as it exits point B. As you recover your palm low over the water you form an elliptical pattern to put with your other hand at point A. Then reverse the pattern to take your hand back over the top of the water to where it exited from. Repeat this half elliptical pattern above the water to learn by sight and feel, the elbow bend, and extend the hand and arm from your shoulder into point A.

Keep your head above water to see and feel what you are doing to recover your palm flat over the top of the water. You shorten the radius of rotation by going directly from where your hand exits to see your entry into that imaginary hole you do in your face float. This means you do not have to lift your arm way out of the water or way around in a circular pattern. You simply take your hand out and put it in a short pattern.

Be certain to observe that your palm is flat upon exit as you finish your stroke by rolling your shoulder and upper arm back. This action will rotate your palm flat upon exit, and let you recover your elbow and hand directly over your ear. If your shoulder is still down you will not be able to rotate your palm flat, and this can lead to shoulder problems later.

55 PIVOT STEP

Standing in waist deep water, use your non breathing side foot as your pivot foot and step forward on to your breathing side foot. As you step forward bring your arm around in the recovery as you just learned how to do, and place your hand in the water in the hole where both hands and arms are fully extended in the neutral position face float. This is the same identical element you learned when you practiced streamlining stretching out on the bed with your forehead down on the mattress and your arms and legs stretched out together.

Your hand will start to follow the pattern of the imaginary midline plane that centers down the middle of your body from your head to your feet. Note that as your hips roll with your shoulder roll, your hand and arm will pass by your rotated hip as it clears for you to finish your stroke like completing a push-up to extend your arm. Finish your stroke by rolling your shoulder back which will rotate your forearm and palm flat to begin the recovery. Now you are ready to step forward again, repeat the stroke, and feel the water pressure on your hand and forearm to gain propulsion and swim while floating.

Focus on feeling the water pressure on your hand and forearm. You'll need to feel this pressure when you start swimming to be efficient.

56 RELAX AND RELEASE YOUR ARMS TO LET THEM FLOAT UP TO THE TOP ON THEIR OWN

Use your mind to control your body parts in space to know how to relax as well as flex your muscles. Squat down in the water up to your shoulders, and put your arms at your sides. Hold your arms down briefly, and then release your muscles so that your arms will bend and float up to the surface level with your shoulders. Experience the idea that your body parts float to understand that your body can float equally as well. All you need to do is inflate your lungs like a balloon.

57 INHALE AND EXHALE TO FEEL YOUR BODY FLOAT UP AND SINK DOWN

Squat down up to your shoulders using your legs as shock absorbers bending your knees and slowly exhale to allow your body torso to start to sink up to your neck and your mouth. Then stop your sinking with your legs and start to slowly inhale to feel your torso and body start to float back up. Repeat this action several times so that you can experience flotation when you fill your lungs with air. This will build your confidence to know that if you inflate your lungs, it will be very difficult for you to sink.

Floating Principles

58 HOW ARCHIMEDES' PRINCIPLE WORKS FOR YOU

Archimedes demonstrated that you are buoyed up by a force equal to the amount of the weight of the water you displace. Thus, when you inflate your lungs you displace more water to provide a greater force to help you float. Fat tissue also weighs less than muscle tissue to displace more water to help you float. However, fat cannot contract like muscle to be a propulsive force.

59 NEWTON'S THIRD LAW OF MOTION - ACTION-REACTION

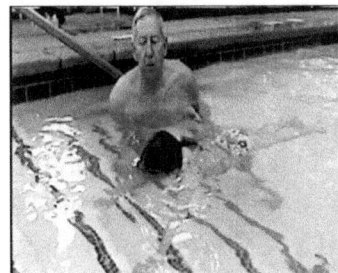

Newton's Third Law states that for every action there is an equal and opposite reaction. While floating, if your head weighs 16 pounds and is above the water line, then 16 pounds of force must go down below your belly button or center of gravity. This means your legs and hips will drop down if you lift your head and shoulders up out of the water. This is highly inefficient because you are technically not floating and allowing Archimedes' principle to work for you.

Your head controls your body position.

Take the time to observe how most adults swim. Many did not master their breathing as students and now swim with their head out of water all of the time. This proves highly exhausting and can get you into trouble in a hurry. This book and video series teach you how to easily master your breathing skills to be more efficient. I want you to enjoy an active lifestyle and maintain a secure environment.

60 BERNOULLI'S PRINCIPLE - BODY LIFT AND PROPULSION

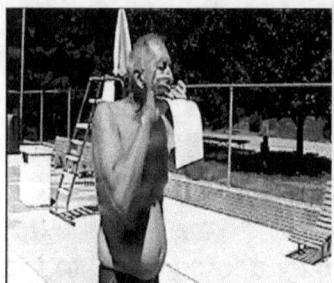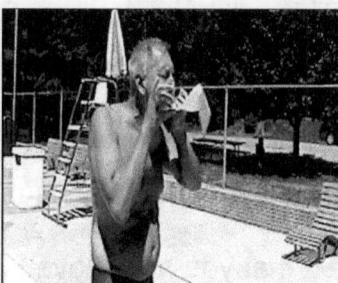

Bernoulli's Principle states that when there is a constriction to a stream of air or water, the speed of flow will increase. If you make your body position face float look like an airplane wing, water molecules take longer to go over the top of your body and are constricted. Other water molecules speed up to fill the gap underneath you and give you slight lift. Your arm position in the freestyle pull works the same way when you feel water pressure on your hand and forearm.

When you perform your face float in the neutral position with your arms and legs fully extended, focus on trying to suck your stomach in a little so that you bend over or slightly pike at your waist. This will cause your body to look like an airplane wing, and get a certain amount of lift to keep you on top of the water efficiently. Once you start to belly out or bend backward at the waist, your head and shoulders typically rise up and your hips go down to create excessive amounts of drag or resistance to become highly inefficient.

In succeeding steps I explain how Bernoulli's principle is applied to your freestyle arm stroke and your breaststroke kick to give you maximum propulsive force. I don't believe many swimming instructors have heard of Bernoulli or how to apply this very important physics principle I learned from Doc Counsilman.

61 MORE DISTANCE PER STROKE OR DPS

When you take longer strokes while floating, you have more time to exhale and inhale and swim continuously replacing your air supply as you use it up. If you take short choppy strokes, you burn up your air supply faster, and you do not allow enough time to replace your air. This will cause you to create an oxygen debt, and you'll have to stop swimming at some point which can cause you to get into trouble with a depleted air supply.

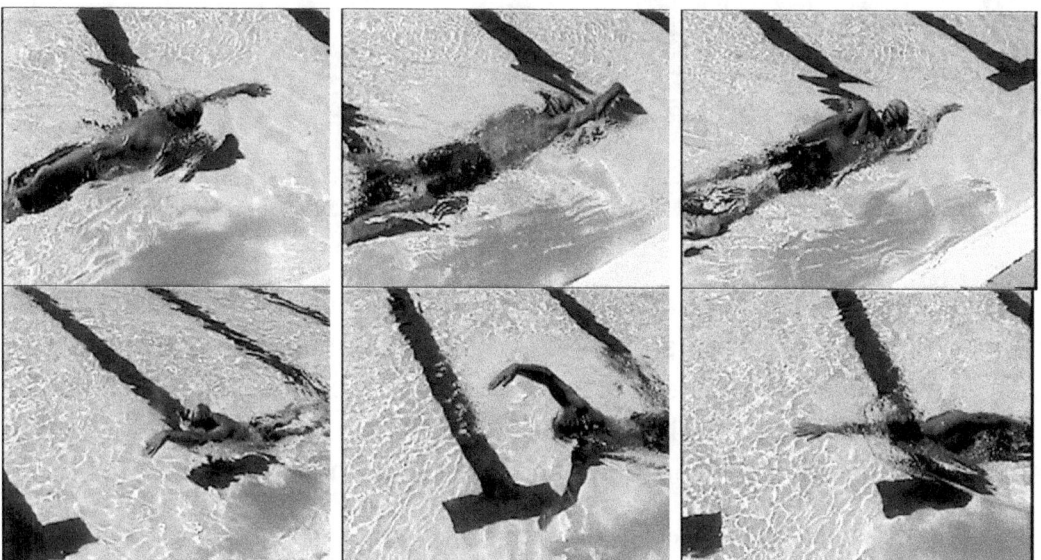

The DPS or distance per stroke concept is how you can swim farther and faster, and use up the least amount of energy. This book and companion video series teach you how to be efficient for recreational, fitness, and competitive swimming.

If you work out to improve your cardiovascular conditioning, then apply more force to expend more effort in shorter distances and allow more time to rest in between repeats. Your oxygen debt will increase accordingly, and your body will adapt to that level of conditioning.

As you get older you lose muscle tissue and flexibility, and you have to learn to reduce resistance and increase your range of motion to improve your efficiency. If you are a competitor, the key is to maintain your body position with the proper pace. If your stroke falls apart at the end of your race, you lose.

62 FACE DOWN, HOLD YOUR BREATH FOR 10 TO 20 SECONDS

 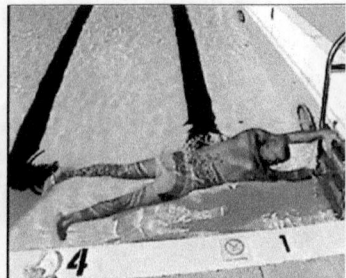 

Where you have steps at varying heights leading into the pool you can use the step just underwater to place your hands and extend your legs out. Put your face down in the water to raise your legs up and achieve the neutral face float position. If steps are not available, you can use the ladder step just below the waterline in the shallow end of the pool.

Know that your face must go down into the water to face float in order for your legs and torso to be level on the surface. If your legs are dropping, lower your face and torso to raise your legs up. Keep working on mastering this step to understand this floating process.

63 FACE FLOAT TO STAND UP POSITION

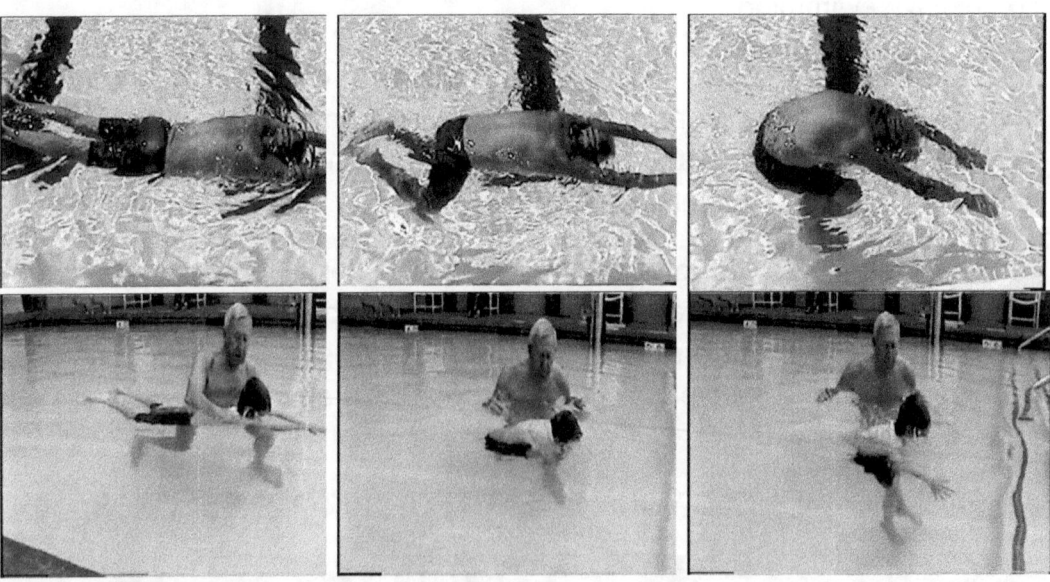

Hold onto the top of the gutter or the ladder step just below the waterline. Once level floating face down, bring your knees up to your shoulders to rotate your hips. With goggles you see your feet directly below you to stand up. Do this prior to using up your air supply.

Master this skill now next to the wall. Very soon you will do a face float away from the wall, and you'll need to stop and stand up in the open water without any assist from holding onto the wall.

64 TURTLE FLOAT 10-20 SECONDS

Bend your knees to lower your upper body in the water up to the tops of your shoulders. Slowly bend your head and face into the water and gently lift your feet and legs up off the bottom. As you bring your knees up to your shoulders, reach your arms around both legs to hold them up to your chest to float freely. Your body will tilt forward so that the rounded part of your back will float to the surface. Be sure to hold your breath long enough to experience this float.

You can master this step more easily if you wear your goggles to see your legs come up and your arms grasp around them holding your arms together. Focus on tucking your head down and not raise it up to relax. Then feel yourself floating on top of the water. To stand up again, release your legs and put your feet on the pool bottom.

65 FLOAT IN THE WALL BRACE 5, 10, 15, 20 SECONDS

To help you keep your legs up to float, you can make a wall brace with your hands and arms extended while holding onto the pool wall. Use your non dominant arm to grasp the top of the pool lip or gutter. Take your other breathing side hand and rotate your fingers clockwise so they face down in the water and place your hand flat against the wall approximately 6 or 8 inches directly below your top hand.

Now you can extend your body away from the wall and exert leverage with your hands and arms to help assist keeping your body in a level floating position. From this position you can turn your face to practice breathing or work on your kick.

To feel floating you can slowly and gently lift your hands up away from the wall. Start holding your breath now at least 15 to 20 seconds with each trial. This will make it easier for you to float and do a push off from the wall in coming steps.

66 DEMONSTRATE HOW WHEN YOUR HEAD GOES UP YOUR HIPS GO DOWN - NEWTON'S THIRD LAW OF MOTION - ACTION-REACTION

In the wall brace position lower your head and face in the water, and moderately push against the wall with your lower hand to boost your legs up to float level. Then lift your head and shoulders up out of the water, and see what happens to your hips and legs. You will note that your legs and hips go downward rapidly to create resistance. This is why it is very inefficient to try to swim with your head out of the water the whole time that quickly leads to exhaustion and potential drowning.

Start to practice placing your face in the water and holding your breath longer so that your legs will remain level. Now you can easily kick to keep your feet up and be much more efficient. With a moderate kick holding your breath longer, you can easily add your breathing to help you swim continuously for longer distances replacing your air supply as you go.

67 FLOAT LEVEL HEAD DOWN RELAXING YOUR WALL GRIP

To experience what it's like to float freely, you must slowly relax your grip on the wall after you first get your body position level on top of the water without having to kick your feet. This will require you to push against the wall with your lower hand to boost your legs up together.

Once you are relaxed on the wall, put your face completely in the water so that your ears are wet. Extend your arms away from the wall as far as you can, but maintain slight contact with the wall. Gently raise your top hand slightly up off the wall, but not too high. Otherwise, when some weight goes up out of the water, some weight on your other end must go down, and you will not maintain your body position to use the water to help you to float.

68 CHILD GUIDANCE - HOLD THEM UNDER THEIR ARMPITS (NEVER AT THEIR WAIST EXCEPT IN THE WALL BRACE POSITION)

If you hold your child by the waist or center of gravity, he will feel like an elephant has jumped on his back. He will automatically dog paddle to try to force his head and shoulders up out of the water. This is not a good response to condition if you are trying to teach him how to float.

Hold him under his armpits and tell him to put his head down and feel his ears between his upper arms. He should also feel his legs together, and his toes pointed. This is the neutral face float position, and his starting and stopping point if he ever gets lost performing his strokes or floating. If his strokes look uncoordinated, then go back to the neutral face float position and start the progressive sequence all over again.

69 FLOAT IN WALL BRACE AND DO MODERATE KICK 1-2-1-2

 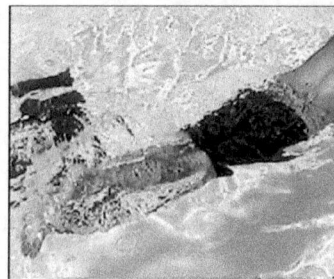 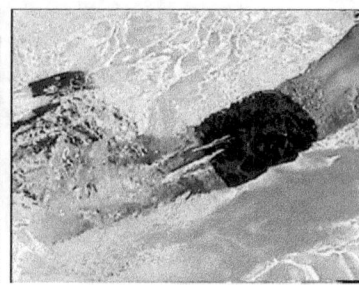

From the wall brace position in a level body position, start a very moderate kick keeping the rhythm by counting in your head or to your pupil 1-2-1-2. You do not have to have your face in the water when you do this kick, but it helps to put your face in the water and/or use your leverage to keep your feet up to do the kick in a very moderate rhythm.

Do not overpower your kick and waste a lot of energy that will not give you as great a propulsive force as your arms. Focus on keeping your ankles together and transferring the same identical element you did when you were kicking on top of your mattress at home. Your ankles will be relaxed with your toes slightly pointed to kick at the water surface.

70 BUCKET KICK ONLY YOUR ANKLES UP AND DOWN AT THE SURFACE

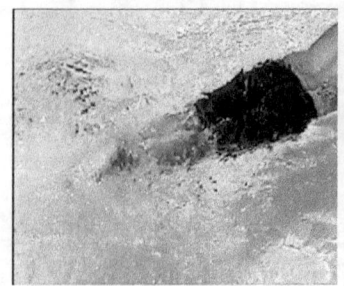 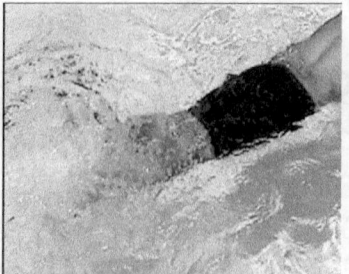 

Imagine kicking your ankles inside a 5 gallon bucket one foot in diameter. Your focus will be on your ankles kicking up and down together for 6 to 8 inches of separation. Relax your ankles and kick at the surface, but do not overly beat the water.

71 REPEAT THE BUCKET KICK BLOWING BIG BUBBLES WITH YOUR HEAD TURNING TO INHALE ON THE SIDE OF YOUR LOWER ARM

Your lower arm is bent and out of the way to allow your face to turn without hitting your arm. This is the beginning of learning how to turn your head to exhale your air and take another breath to swim continuously. Do a moderate kick to keep your feet on top of the water to focus more on rolling your head and shoulders up to breathe.

After you take a breath, place your face directly back down in the water and start to exhale large bubbles immediately. Feel the bubbles coming up and around your cheeks. You only need to exhale about 20% of your air supply while you are kicking and getting ready to turn your head and shoulders up for your next breath. Make this a smooth process that you can keep repeating.

72 CHILD GUIDANCE - FISHING ROD FLIP

 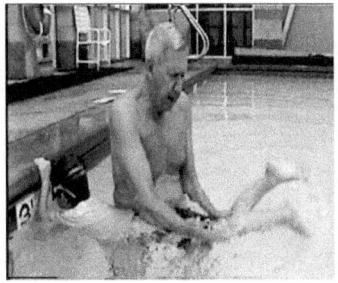 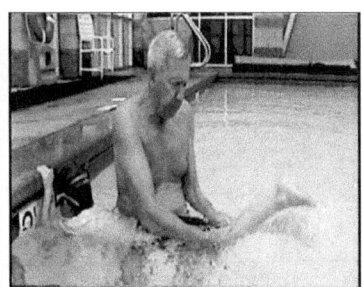

After your child gets in the wall brace position and begins a moderate kick, stand beside him, and place two of your fingers above and below his kneecaps. Use your thumb like a stop on a fishing rod to prevent his lower leg from lifting up too high out of the water.

By alternately using your thumb to press his calf back down, you can help him learn a moderate rhythm. This will guide him to learn this important motor pattern. Make sure he maintains contact with the wall so he can focus on his kick in the wall brace position. You don't want his brain to start processing other information if he lets go of the wall.

Step 7 Learn how to stand up from neutral floating position

73 REVIEW NEUTRAL POSITION FACE FLOAT

Earlier you learned how to float in the arm brace position against the wall. You could float freely by placing your hands just below the waterline on one of the concrete steps leading into the shallow end or a step on the ladder. In those positions it was like lying on your mattress with your arms and legs fully extended together. You placed your forehead down on the mattress to get spatial awareness so that your legs would remain level when you practiced in the shallow end.

You also learned how to hold your breath for 15 to 20 seconds. This gives you enough time to do a push off, glide, and float without using up all of your air supply before you have to stand up. In waist deep water where you can stand up at any time, maintain this streamlined neutral position. This is your start and finish point for every continuous stroke. Always remember that you are floating with your mouth open and stomach sucked in to bend over slightly at your waist to keep your legs up. Relax and focus on feeling the water buoy you up while staying balanced to avoid rolling over.

74 REVIEW FACE FLOAT TO STAND UP POSITION

 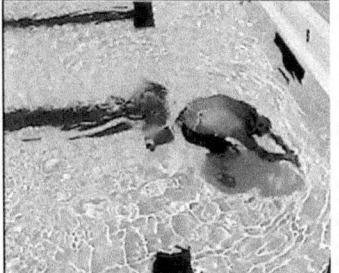 

Practice in the shallow end in waist deep water. Toward the end of your face float and before you run out of air, bring your knees up to your shoulders. Wear your goggles and see that your feet will easily rotate below your body for you to stand up. Take time to wait for your hips to rotate downward as your legs come forward in a tuck position. Then extend your legs so your feet contact the pool bottom and stand up. You should have enough air supply so that you do not have to suck in your first breath of air.

75 REVIEW ONE OR TWO FOOT WALL PUSH OFF

With your back up against the wall, place the ball of one foot on the wall and your other foot ahead of you on the bottom. Bend your knees to lower your body, and put your chest in the water. In one motion take a breath, place your face down between your arms, and gently push off with one foot and bring your bottom foot up to float on top of the water. This action will look like you are trying to skim your body on top of the water as opposed to thrusting it out over the top which will cause you to go under like a dive.

76 PUSH OFF AND GLIDE FOR DISTANCE 10-20 SECONDS

It's really important that you master this streamlining skill to keep your legs on the surface so you can glide farther and farther with each attempt. Suck in your stomach to bend over slightly at your waist. Stretch out your arms and legs together pointing your toes to be more streamlined and look like an airplane wing. You can learn to keep your legs and feet up with practice. In your glide you can force your upper body downward to help keep your legs and feet up level. If your legs are sinking, it is because you have not forced your head down to look directly at the bottom. You may still be looking forward under the water too much.

Work on your streamlining at the same time by making sure that one hand is securely held on top of the other hand, and that your upper arms squeeze your ears and your toes are pointed with your legs together. Be sure to reward yourself for being able to make longer and longer glides on one breath. This will make it much easier for you to swim with efficient strokes.

77 PUSH OFF THE BOTTOM AND GLIDE BACK TO THE WALL - KEEP YOUR FINGERS UP TO AVOID JAMMING YOUR FINGERS

  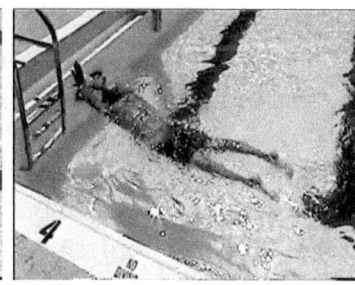

Rather than walk back and waste practice time, use your pivot foot to step forward after you squat down to put your chest in the water. Push off the bottom with your lead foot, and glide back to the wall. Curl your fingers up a little bit when your hands are together to not jam your fingers on the wall. Keep your face looking down at the bottom, and use the top of your vision with your goggles to see the wall coming.

Step 8 Arms stroking progressive sequence

78 WALKING ON THE BOTTOM EYES FIXED ON AN OBJECT

You want to transfer to the pool all of the same identical elements you learned standing in front of your dressing room mirror at home. Pick out an object on the wall to fix your eyes on and keep your brain from processing extra information. Focus on one specific body part at a time.

Move away from the wall several feet and begin using your windmill arm pulls keeping your hands and arms opposite and head steady, and walk directly toward that object. Repeat several times until you can do this without moving your head, and feel the water pressure on your hands and forearms. You can repeat bending your knees to lower your body in the water up to your armpits.

79 WALKING ON THE BOTTOM TURNING YOUR HEAD TO BREATHE

Repeat the previous step walking in shallow water with your head out of water to practice exhaling 20% of your air, rolling your shoulders and head to your breathing arm side as you pull your arm by your side. As you finish your stroke and recover your arm out of the water, your upper arm will knock your face back down into your face float position. Except in practice your face is still not in the water, but will turn to look back towards that object on the wall.

Do not look to the other side; only look directly back at that object on the wall. Then focus on lifting your non-breathing arm up and over the water. Wait to start turning your head until the non-breathing arm enters the water up to your wrist. This will improve your timing for your breathing by giving you a little more time to exhale the 20% of your air supply. If you exhale only 20%, you still have 80% left to float. Please keep your mouth open and relaxed the whole time.

80 STAND IN PLACE AND DO THE CHICKEN WING SHOULDER LIFT AND ROLL

Place your hands on the tops of your shoulders for feedback to know if your shoulders are turning, rolling, and opposite of one another. Focus on that wall object and make sure that your shoulders roll, turn, and lift one on top of the other but remain completely opposite of each other at all times.

81 WALKING IN WITH CHICKEN WING KEEPING YOUR HEAD STEADY

Repeat the previous step only this time walk toward that wall object. Keep your head steady to maintain your balance and body position. Visualize your body roll or rotation about that imaginary rod that we talked about before that runs from your head to your toes through your body.

82 STAND IN PLACE SHOULDER LIFT AND ROLL TO ARM EXTENSION

Keep your eyes fixed on that object to keep your head steady. Start with your breathing side to lift your shoulder and arm up and around. Keep that shoulder high so that you can see it clearly in your vision and almost feel your shoulder touching your cheek. Keep your shoulder high, and extend your shoulder and arm another 6" over the water as far as you can before your hand enters. Keep a slight bend in your elbow. Your efficiency improves with more distance per stroke to take fewer strokes.

83 PIVOT STEP WITH CHICKEN WING FOR SHOULDER LIFT, AND ROLL INTO ARM EXTENSION

The pivot step forward is more like the identical element of swimming to help you visualize getting more distance per stroke. Instead of just putting your hand in the water in front of your face before you roll your shoulder down after you take a breath or for any stroke, focus on keeping your shoulder high to extend your reach with your hand as far forward as possible before entering the water.

Like you did in front of the dressing mirror, your non breathing side foot is your pivot foot to step forward and backward with your dominant breathing side foot. Focus on your shoulder lift just prior to your entry. Finish your stroke as if you were doing a push-up. When you roll your shoulder back to complete your stroke, it will rotate your forearm and turn your palm flat. Keep your palm flat in the recovery and directly to your entry. Look at your pattern to condition the visual with the kinesthetic feeling so that when you are swimming you will feel the finish, roll, and keep your palm flat in the recovery.

84 PIVOT STEP WITH NON-BREATHING SIDE SHOULDER LIFT, ROLL, AND ARM EXTENSION

Change your pivot foot and repeat the previous step. Keep your head steady to focus on completing your non breathing side stroke. You have to focus on rolling that side up, too, to roll your forearm and palm flat on the recovery. This technique avoids painful rotator cuff shoulder problems, and improves the timing for your breathing learning to lift your arm around and making a better entry into your catch position.

85 PIVOT STEP NON-BREATHING SIDE LIFT, ROLL, AND EXTENSION

Practice feeling the water pressure on your hand and forearm as you pivot your body and foot backward. This will help you emphasize your shoulder roll and lift of your arms in the recovery. Mastery of these early steps will help you to swim efficiently very soon when we will start a sequence of steps from the face float neutral position in a push off from the wall.

Freestyle Arm Progression –
your hand follows the midline in the neutral position

86 CATCH - HANDS ENTER FINGERTIPS FIRST WITH WRIST SLIGHTLY FLEXED

It is not necessary to cup your hand or squeeze your fingers together. But you must enter the water fingertips first with your wrists slightly flexed and preferably in the hole. The hole is where you had your hands together and arms stretched out on your mattress to gain spatial awareness for the neutral position face float.

Use your goggles to see how and where your hand actually enters. Immediately after you enter the water in your catch, start to feel the water pressure on your hand and forearm as you depress and pull your hand following the imaginary midline.

87 ROTATION – REACH OVER THE BARREL BRINGING YOUR HAND DIRECTLY BELOW YOUR ELBOW

This motion is like reaching over a barrel while maintaining your alignment with that imaginary rod through your body. Rotate your hand and forearm directly below your elbow, and feel the water pressure build on your hand and forearm. Focus on pulling yourself forward as if you were holding onto a rope stretched underwater beneath you. The object is to hold on to as much water as possible, and pull and push yourself forward to gain more propulsive force with your early rotation.

If you don't feel water pressure on your hand and forearm, you are probably dropping your elbows to slide your hand and forearms through the water. You will feel like you are swimming hard, but your body will not go forward. You are like a car spinning its wheels on ice. You must feel the water pressure on your hand and forearm. In time when you do each stroke correctly, you will build up your strength and be more efficient taking fewer strokes.

88 FOLLOW THROUGH – HOLD ON TO THE WATER AND PULL AND PUSH YOUR WAY THROUGH

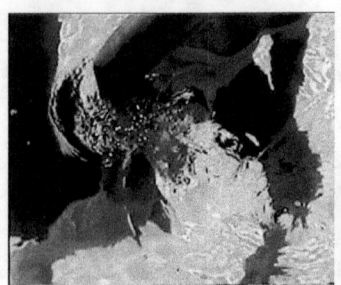 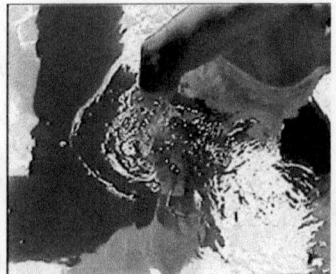 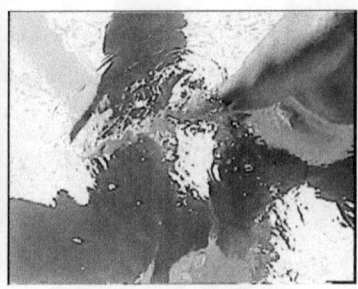

It is far better to take a few good strokes than a lot of fast poor ones. To conserve your energy and not run out of your air supply, you must make good efficient long strokes as described in the two previous steps. Check to see whether or not you are moving efficiently through the water and floating level without having to use much energy. This is the true test of your efficiency. You don't need an instructor to tell you that.

89 RECOVERY - LIFT YOUR ARM UP AND ROTATE THE PALM FLAT TO EXIT FROM THE WATER IN A STRAIGHT LINE INTO YOUR CATCH POSITION

As was explained earlier in step 84, to practice your recovery (one arm at a time), squat down up to your shoulders and watch what your palm is doing moving your hand forward and backward all above water to condition the recovery pattern. Imagine your entry is point A and your exit as point B. You can bend your arm to keep your palm flat and move in a straight line forward and then reverse. Condition the pattern to master what you see and feel your hand and arm perform so you can copy this same motion when you swim and aren't able to see your recovery.

90 ARM STROKING AT THE WALL - AT A 45° ANGLE

To continue with your freestyle arm progression, stand at the wall at a 45° angle to avoid hitting the wall with your stroking hand. Place your non-breathing side hand on the wall, squat down up to your chest, place your ear on your lead arm, and roll your head up to simulate breathing as you stroke standing in place. Practice your catch and rotation first with your face out of the water, and then in the water. See what you should be doing to get feedback to teach yourself to do it correctly. Focus on keeping your ear in contact with your upper arm to roll instead of lifting up your head which would cause your legs to drop and be inefficient when swimming.

Practice and master these same identical elements to perform when you start to swim. Your mastery is entirely up to you. If you perform each individual step very well, you will swim very well also.

Pool Edge Progression

91 FREESTYLE ARM STROKING HAND AND ARM IN THE WATER

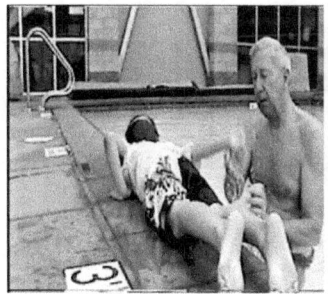 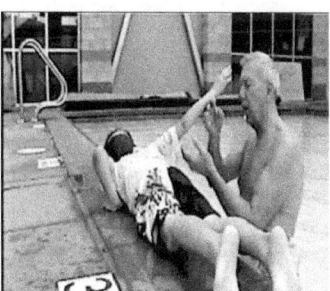 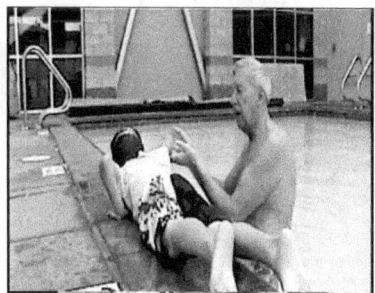

Lie down on the top step or side of the pool to practice stroking your arm in the water to feel the water pressure on your hand and forearm. Roll on your non-breathing side to lift your shoulder, arm and hand on your breathing side. Your body rolls about that imaginary rod to keep your alignment.

First make your catch and rotation, then focus on feeling the water pressure as you pull your arm backward. Your immediate feedback is if you are in the correct position, you will feel more water pressure on your hand and forearm. Your body is out of the water to see your pulling pattern throughout the entire pattern including recovery. Make a mental image of this pattern to copy when you swim.

92 ALTERNATE OTHER ARM BY TURNING YOUR BODY AROUND

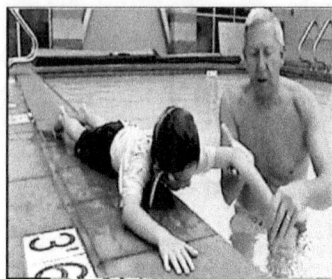
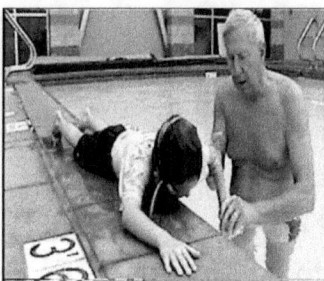
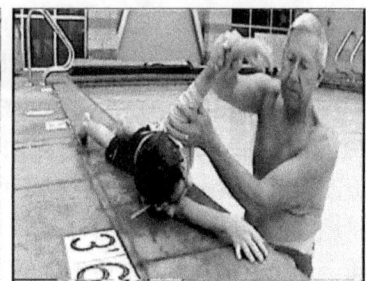

Practice with your non breathing side arm as well. Focus on rolling about your lead arm so that you can lift your shoulder, and recover your arm to place in the catch and rotation for the next stroke. Beginners forget they have to roll the non-breathing side up to recover that arm the same as their breathing side. The arm will not recover all by itself. You have to focus on that action.

93 CHILD GUIDANCE - PROVIDING SLIGHT RESISTANCE TO FEEL THE PATTERN

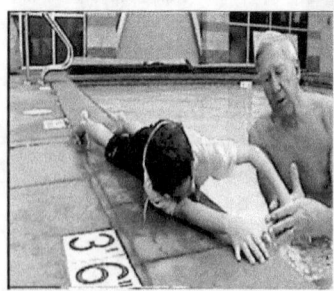
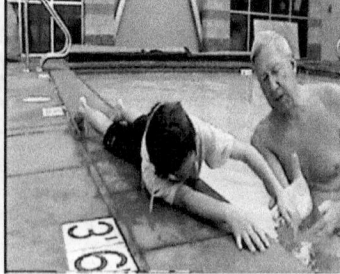
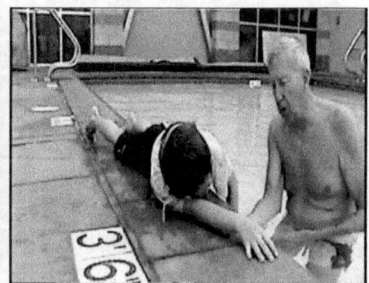

With your child lying on the side of the pool, place your hand under his hand to provide guidance and resistance throughout the entire pattern. Be sure to practice on both sides. If you have a small child this is much like what you did in the bathtub. If he does not keep constant pressure on your hand and forearm, you can clasp your thumb around his hand to hold it in place. Explain that you are resisting him to feel the pressure just as he will when he is actually swimming.

94 PUSH OFF THE WALL, GLIDE AND ADD MODERATE BUCKET KICK TO STAND UP POSITION

Start your push off and get your body float position. Add a very moderate bucket kick, continue for 15 to 20 seconds, and stand up. Mark your distance on the wall or on the bottom, and repeat trying to exceed that distance each time. This will help you focus on your streamlining and body position to be efficient.

95 PUSH OFF THE BOTTOM, GLIDE, ADD MODERATE KICK BACK TO THE WALL

Continue your practice going back to the wall instead of walking back and pushing off the wall again. This doubles your practice time to gain valuable feedback maintaining your body position and doing a moderate kick for propulsion.

96 PUSH OFF THE WALL, GLIDE, MODERATELY KICK ON YOUR SIDE, AND ADD ONE ARM STROKING

In this variation you'll repeat the previous steps only you will stroke starting with your breathing side arm first. Your non-breathing side arm will remain in the face float position on that side the whole time. Focus on keeping your ear on that upper arm like you did in the wall stroking steps. As you stroke with your breathing arm, focus on your catch and early rotation to feel more water pressure on your hand and forearm. Your moderate kick to keep your legs together and feet on top should be mastered so well you no longer have to think about it.

Keep focusing on previous steps such as catch, rotation, and follow through into your recovery. This is your opportunity to view your stroke above and below the water. This feedback teaches you the correct technique.

97 PUSH OFF THE BOTTOM, MODERATELY KICK ON YOUR SIDE, AND DO YOUR OTHER ARM STROKING BACK TO THE WALL

To gain valuable practice time, do not walk back. Practice kicking and swimming with your non-breathing side arm only, but keep your head down looking at the bottom. Focus on your catch, rotation and follow through into your recovery to make sure that you roll your shoulder up and lift your hand around palm flat to place in the water for your next stroke.

98 PUSH OFF THE WALL, ADD YOUR KICK, TAKE 2-3 LONG SLOW STROKES ALTERNATING YOUR ARMS WITH NO BREATHING

You want to think about good stroke mechanics. You do not have to breathe, and you already know how to make your catch, rotation, and follow through into your recovery to complete a good stroke on each arm. All you have to do now is maintain your face float and keep your hands and arms opposite to <u>place</u> your hands in the water in the hole.

Focus on floating first with a good glide, and keeping your legs together with a moderate kick. This gives you plenty of time to focus on doing correct arm strokes with each arm. You have your goggles on to see how and where each hand enters the water. Look for early rotation and watch your hand pull in that imaginary midline underneath you. Your head may look back to see how you finish your pull since you are not breathing to maintain your streamlined body position.

99 PUSH OFF THE BOTTOM, ADD YOUR KICK, AND TAKE 2-3 LONG SLOW STROKES BACK TO THE WALL

This adds to your practice going back to the wall. Keep your eyes open to see the wall and not crash into it. Follow the same mechanics as you did in the previous step. Focus on keeping your forehead down a little more, but you can still look forward by rolling your eyes up.

100 PUSH OFF AND GLIDE FOR DISTANCE 30-40 SECONDS TO MASTER FLOATING FEEDBACK SKILLS

Glide and stretch out your body a little longer with each push off. Suck in your stomach to bend slightly at your waist. This greatly improves your spatial awareness for streamlining and floating. Mark a visual point on the wall to use as your goal to outdistance on your next attempt. You may think you are not moving, but keep looking at the bottom to see that you are still moving very slowly. If you can continue to hold your breath a little bit longer, you'll learn more about streamlining your body to apply then while swimming without kicking to keep your feet up.

101   PUSH OFF AND GLIDE, ADD YOUR KICK, AND ROLL UP YOUR BREATHING SIDE TO DO ONE ARM STROKING

This step helps you master your breathing arm stroke technique. Keep your non-breathing arm fixed in the face float position, and rotate your head resting your ear on that upper arm. By having mastered your floating skills, your brain now has more time to focus on taking good strokes to feel the water pressure on your hand and forearm to get maximum propulsion. Notice how well you move directly forward with each stroke. If you move very little, it shows you are not using good technique. Focus more on good rotation like reaching over a barrel starting to pull yourself forward when you stroke back. Remember to pull and push yourself forward with that one arm stroke, rolling your body, and keeping your legs together to kick moderately.

102   PUSH OFF AND GLIDE, ADD YOUR KICK, BUT KEEP YOUR HEAD FIXED LOOKING STRAIGHT AHEAD AND ROLL UP YOUR NON-BREATHING SIDE ARM TO STROKE

Often in swimming lessons, the focus will be on just your breathing side arm. You forget to roll up your non breathing side with your shoulder high to easily recover your arm to start your next stroke. This causes you to drag your arm around instead of lifting it over the top of the water to improve your efficiency.

Focus on keeping your head steady as if that imaginary rod is still running from your head to your toes. You do not turn your head to your non-breathing side; you look straight ahead while this arm strokes and recovers. This helps you to maintain your streamlining and body position to float. The object is to pull and push your body forward through the water while floating, and not to thrash and press your hands downward to keep your head above water.

103   PUSH OFF AND GLIDE, KICK, AND ADD ALTERNATING ARMS BUT COUNT YOUR STROKES FOR 30-40 SECONDS

You can easily count your right arm strokes by odd or even numbers to get a total arm stroke count. If in a set amount of time and distance you find that you take more strokes than are necessary, you can focus on being more efficient by making better strokes to take fewer of them on your next trial. This helps you to conserve your energy, and use your floating skills to help you swim efficiently.

104   PUSH OFF THE WALL, GLIDE AND ADD MODERATE BUCKET KICK TO STAND UP POSITION

Start your push off and get your body float position. Add a very moderate bucket kick, continue for 15 to 20 seconds, and stand up. Mark your distance on the wall or on the bottom, and repeat trying to exceed that distance each time. This will help you focus on your streamlining and body position to be efficient.

105   PUSH OFF THE BOTTOM, GLIDE, ADD MODERATE KICK BACK TO THE WALL

Continue your practice going back to the wall instead of walking back and pushing off the wall again. This doubles your practice time to gain valuable feedback maintaining your body position and doing a moderate kick for propulsion.

106 PUSH OFF THE WALL, GLIDE, MODERATELY KICK ON YOUR SIDE, AND ADD ONE ARM STROKING

In this variation you'll repeat the previous steps only you will stroke starting with your breathing side arm first. Your non-breathing side arm will remain in the face float position on that side the whole time. Focus on keeping your ear on that upper arm like you did in the wall stroking steps. As you stroke with your breathing arm, focus on your catch and early rotation to feel more water pressure on your hand and forearm. Your moderate kick to keep your legs together and feet on top should be mastered so well you no longer have to think about it.

Keep focusing on previous steps such as catch, rotation, and follow through into your recovery. This is your opportunity to view your stroke above and below the water. This feedback teaches you the correct technique.

107 PUSH OFF THE BOTTOM, MODERATELY KICK ON YOUR SIDE, AND DO YOUR OTHER ARM STROKING BACK TO THE WALL

To gain valuable practice time, do not walk back. Practice kicking and swimming with your non-breathing side arm only, but keep your head down looking at the bottom. Focus on your catch, rotation and follow through into your recovery to make sure that you roll your shoulder up and lift your hand around palm flat to place in the water for your next stroke.

108 PUSH OFF THE WALL, ADD YOUR KICK, TAKE 2-3 LONG SLOW STROKES ALTERNATING YOUR ARMS WITH NO BREATHING

You want to think about good stroke mechanics. You do not have to breathe, and you already know how to make your catch, rotation, and follow through into your recovery to complete a good stroke on each arm. All you have to do now is maintain your face float and keep your hands and arms opposite to <u>place</u> your hands in the water in the hole.

Focus on floating first with a good glide, and keeping your legs together with a moderate kick. This gives you plenty of time to focus on doing correct arm strokes with each arm. You have your goggles on to see how and where each hand enters the water. Look for early rotation and watch your hand pull in that imaginary midline underneath you. Your head may look back to see how you finish your pull since you are not breathing to maintain your streamlined body position.

109 PUSH OFF THE BOTTOM, ADD YOUR KICK, AND TAKE 2-3 LONG SLOW STROKES BACK TO THE WALL

This adds to your practice going back to the wall. Keep your eyes open to see the wall and not crash into it. Follow the same mechanics as you did in the previous step. Focus on keeping your forehead down a little more, but you can still look forward by rolling your eyes up.

110 PUSH OFF AND GLIDE FOR DISTANCE 30-40 SECONDS TO MASTER FLOATING FEEDBACK SKILLS

Glide and stretch out your body a little longer with each push off. Suck in your stomach to bend slightly at your waist. This greatly improves your spatial awareness for streamlining and floating. Mark a visual point on the wall to use as your goal to outdistance on your next attempt. You may think you are not moving, but keep looking at the bottom to see that you are still moving very slowly. If you can continue to hold your breath a little bit longer, you'll learn more about streamlining your body to apply then while swimming without kicking to keep your feet up.

111 PUSH OFF AND GLIDE, ADD YOUR KICK, AND ROLL UP YOUR BREATHING SIDE TO DO ONE ARM STROKING

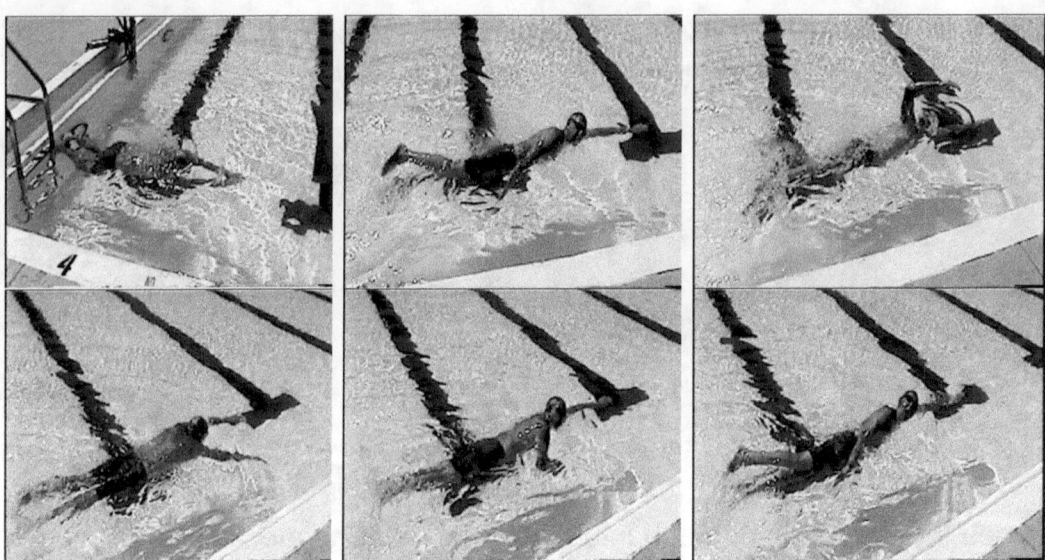

This step helps you master your breathing arm stroke technique. Keep your non-breathing arm fixed in the face float position, and rotate your head resting your ear on that upper arm. By having mastered your floating skills, your brain now has more time to focus on taking good strokes to feel the water pressure on your hand and forearm to get maximum propulsion. Notice how well you move directly forward with each stroke. If you move very little, it shows you are not using good technique. Focus more on good rotation like reaching over a barrel starting to pull yourself forward when you stroke back. Remember to pull and push yourself forward with that one arm stroke, rolling your body, and keeping your legs together to kick moderately.

112 PUSH OFF AND GLIDE, ADD YOUR KICK, BUT KEEP YOUR HEAD FIXED LOOKING STRAIGHT AHEAD AND ROLL UP YOUR NON-BREATHING SIDE ARM TO STROKE

Often in swimming lessons, the focus will be on just your breathing side arm. You forget to roll up your non breathing side with your shoulder high to easily recover your arm to start your next stroke. This causes you to drag your arm around instead of lifting it over the top of the water to improve your efficiency.

  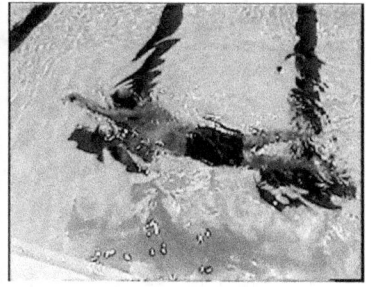

Focus on keeping your head steady as if that imaginary rod is still running from your head to your toes. You do not turn your head to your non-breathing side; you look straight ahead while this arm strokes and recovers. This helps you to maintain your streamlining and body position to float. The object is to pull and push your body forward through the water while floating, and not to thrash and press your hands downward to keep your head above water.

113 PUSH OFF AND GLIDE, KICK, AND ADD ALTERNATING ARMS BUT COUNT YOUR STROKES FOR 30-40 SECONDS

You can easily count your right arm strokes by odd or even numbers to get a total arm stroke count. If in a set amount of time and distance you find that you take more strokes than are necessary, you can focus on being more efficient by making better strokes to take fewer of them on your next trial. This helps you to conserve your energy, and use your floating skills to help you swim efficiently.

Step 9 Standing breathing progressive sequence

114   IMAGINARY ROD HEAD ROLL 2-3 TIMES FACE OUT OF THE WATER - BREATHING SIDE HAND ON YOUR SIDE OR THIGH

With your non-breathing side hand on top of the wall or gutter, place your breathing side hand on your thigh. Now you can focus on an imaginary rod running through your head and body to roll your shoulders and turn your face to practice your breathing while standing in shallow water. Try to keep your ear on your arm instead of lifting your head up and forward. This will help you roll your head as you will when you are actually swimming and breathing.

115   IMAGINARY ROD HEAD ROLL 2-3 TIMES WITH YOUR FACE IN THE WATER - BREATHING SIDE HAND STILL ON YOUR SIDE OR THIGH

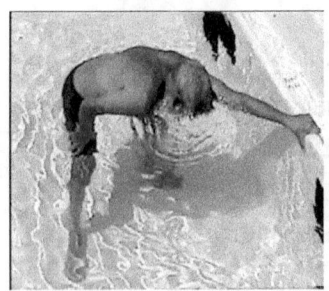  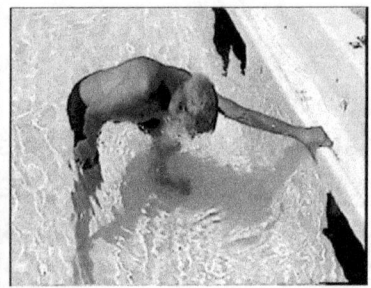

Repeat the previous step with your ear on your arm only this time you will roll your face out of the water and exhale 20% of your air and take enough time to inhale that amount. Then roll your face back down into your face float position, and start to exhale immediately.

116   EXHALE WHEN YOUR FACE GOES BACK DOWN IN THE WATER AND FEEL BIG BUBBLES ON YOUR CHEEKS

As soon as your face rolls back down in the water start to exhale with your mouth relaxed and open perhaps a little wider to blow out big bubbles around your cheeks. You cannot wait to start to exhale as you turn your head; it will be too late. Remember you only need to exhale about 20% of your total air supply. There will be plenty of air left over to help you float and maintain your body position.

117   FACE OUT OF THE WATER SLOW BREATHING AND ARM STROKING WITH YOUR HEAD ROLL

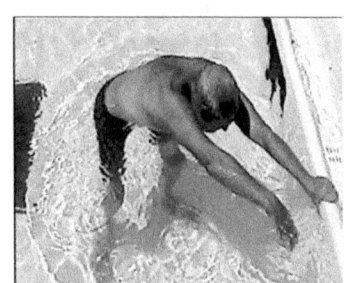  

To see and feel what you are doing, you can take your face out of the water and practice exhaling and inhaling 20% while you are also stroking with your breathing side arm only. This improves the timing of your head roll up to breathe with your arm starting to pull into your catch, rotation, and follow through into your recovery. Your non breathing side hand will still be in contact with the wall while you're standing at a 45° angle to keep your stroking arm and hand from hitting the wall. Make sure that you turn your head up far enough to breathe, and maintain a very long stroke to allow more time to inhale. If you take a very short choppy stroke you will not have enough time to inhale and replace 20% of your air to keep going.

118 FACE IN THE WATER, SLOW BREATHING, AND ARM STROKING WITH YOUR HEAD ROLL

Repeat the previous step and rotate or roll your head up to your side out of the water as you blow large bubbles to exhale and stroke your breathing side arm only. With your non-breathing side hand on the wall, focus on maintaining that imaginary rod and rotating around it. Focus on keeping your ear in contact with your upper arm on your non-breathing side. Remember, if you lift your head up forward, this will cause your hips and legs to go down. After you take your breath, focus on putting your face right back down into your face float position. Do not look up forward or turn your head to the other side. Keep your head steady.

119 IN THE WALL BRACE POSITION DO A MODERATE KICK AT A 45° ANGLE AND ROTATE YOUR HEAD TO BREATHE AND BLOW OUT 20% OF YOUR AIR SUPPLY EACH TIME

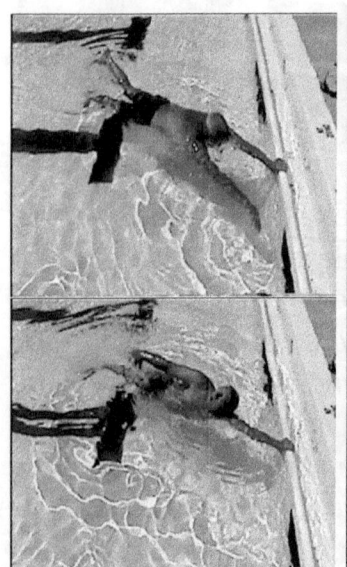 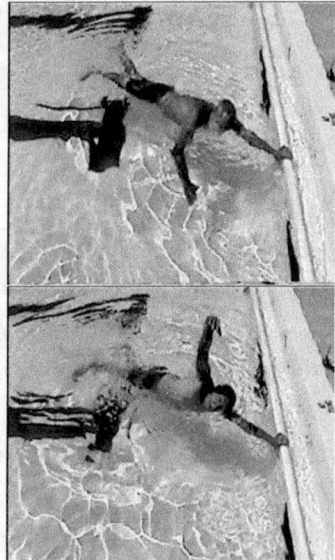 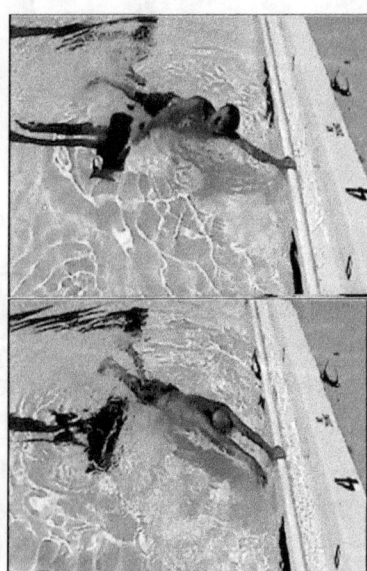

With or without stroking your arm in the wall brace position, practice kicking moderately and rotating your head to breathe as you did previously when you were stroking with one arm only. Note that your lower arm is slightly bent and pressed against the wall for leverage and out of the way when you turn your head to practice your breathing.

Step 10 Swimming and breathing progressive sequence

120   BUCKET KICK ON A KICKBOARD AND PRACTICE ROLLING YOUR HEAD TO BREATHE

Hold the kickboard as you were previously taught. There is a cutout in the lower part of the board for you to place your head. Press down on one side of the board slightly but remain in contact holding it on the sides. Roll your shoulders slightly to turn your head enough to breathe.

121   FREESTYLE ARM STROKING PHRASE

 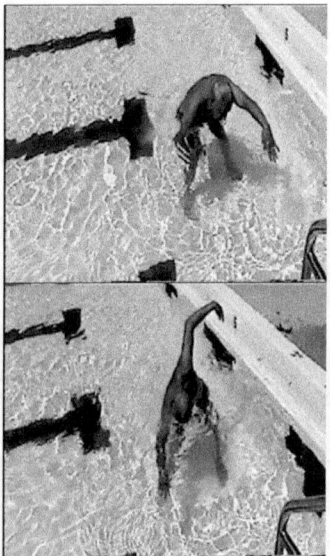 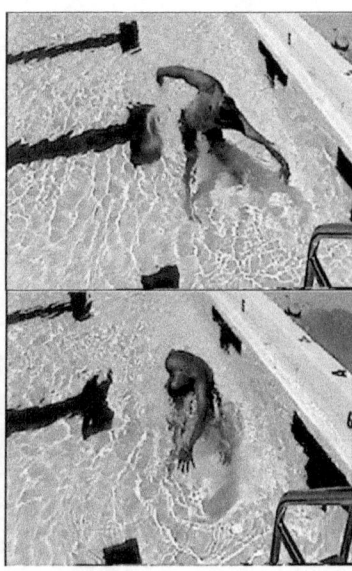

Your brain can focus on an action more easily if you give it a command. Your words trigger when to start the action. To improve your timing, repeat this phrase as you swim. "Pull - take a breath - put your head back down - bring your other arm around."

By saying these words you start those actions and maintain a better rhythm. Focus on taking long strokes, and placing your hands in the water with each stroke. Emphasize your shoulder roll, and keeping your hands and arms opposite. Also focus on looking straight down and slightly ahead after you take your breath, and not to the other side.

You will not start to turn your head to breathe until the non-breathing side hand enters the water. This will improve your timing.

122   FOCUS ON FLOATING FIRST AND STROKING SECOND

You may have learned how to swim a long time ago, and your floating skills need improvement. You may have the mindset to work your arms and legs fairly hard or you will sink. You have now spent a lot of time on floating and adding spatial awareness for one body part at a time. This provides you with success to want to continue to learn new steps.

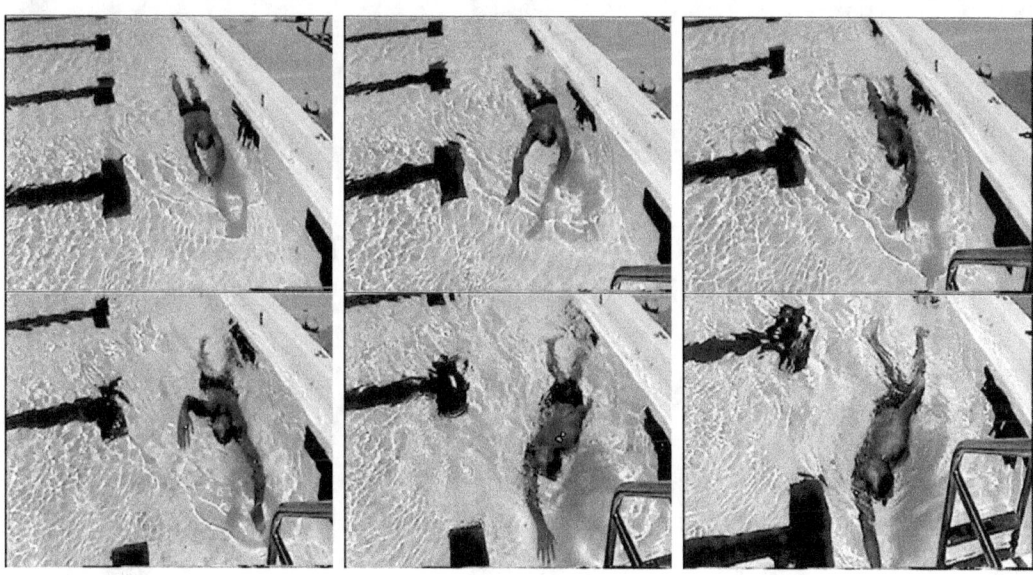

Water is a force you need to understand to help buoy you up and float well. This will help you to conserve your energy and be more efficient.

123   SQUAT DOWN AND SLOWLY WALK WHILE STROKING
ALTERNATE ARMS WITH YOUR BREATHING

Locate an object on the deck or wall to view after you turn your head to take your breath. This prevents you from over rotating your head to the other side; look straight at the bottom. As you walk in, focus on feeling the water pressure on your hands and forearms as you do the rotation immediately after your catch. Make sure that you extend your shoulder forward as well. This will help you to get more distance per stroke and improve your efficiency. You can practice this with your head out of the water and rolling, or squat down enough to put your face back down in the water and blow bubbles.

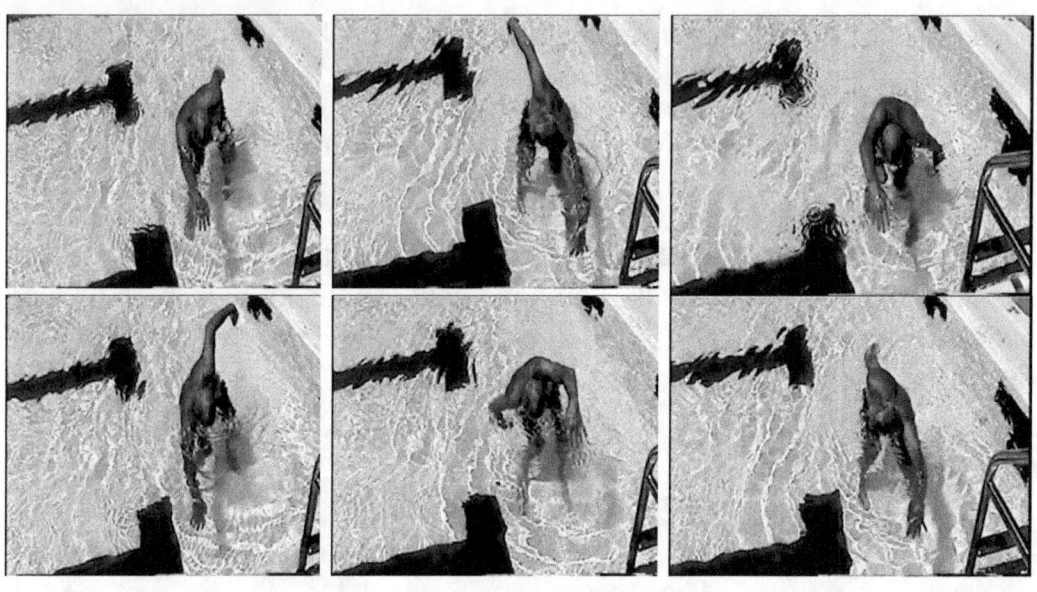

124   LYING ON THE POOL EDGE DO 3-4 BREATHING ARM STROKES IN THE WATER WITH YOUR HEAD ROLL

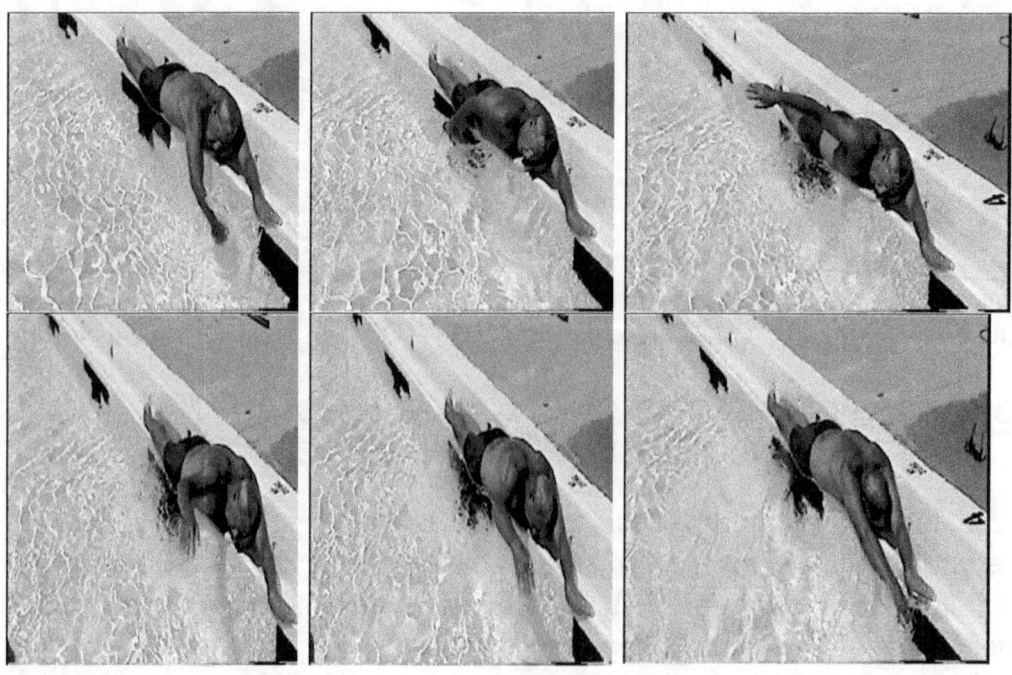

Copy what to do when swimming by lying on the pool edge to get your timing for breathing a little more easily. Feel the water pressure on your hands and forearms as you pull in the water. Make sure that your head is rolling up to exhale and inhale in the right sequence. After you take a breath your arm will come over to knock your face back down in the water. Even though you are lying on a pool deck, try to roll your body on your arm to simulate actual swimming. Then transfer these same identical elements in the water to help you swim out of your glide position and do your breathing.

125 REVIEW YOUR SHOULDER LIFT AND ROLL STROKING YOUR NON-BREATHING SIDE ARM WITH NO HEAD ROLL TO THAT SIDE

You are repeating the previous step only now you're changing sides so you can practice stroking the non-breathing side arm. Be certain to keep your head steady. You must look down at the pool bottom only 4-6 feet ahead instead of forward. This will teach you to maintain your body position while floating. Then transfer the same identical elements to your swimming while keeping your forehead down.

126 DEMONSTRATION OF FREESTYLE WITH BREATHING

  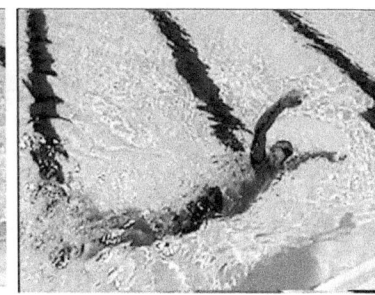

In the sequence of pictures I keep my body alignment rotating around that imaginary rod. I roll my shoulders to recover my hand and place in the hole where both hands are together in the face float neutral position. To breathe, I turn my head keeping my forehead in the water. After I take my breath, I look back down in the water, and start to exhale immediately. My feet are together, and not overly kicking to expend more energy than necessary or create leg drag outside of the midline.

127 PUSH OFF THE WALL, GLIDE, ADD YOUR KICK, AND THEN YOUR ARMS AND START TO EXHALE REPEATING THE PHRASE

  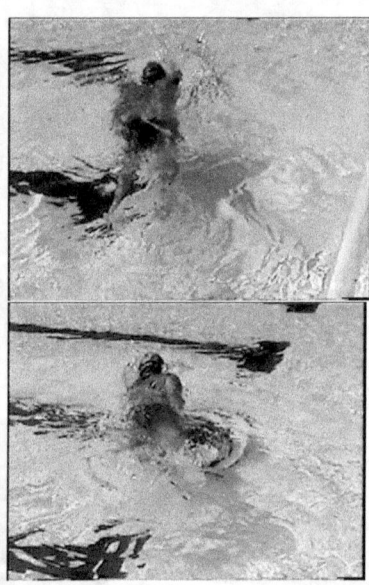

Start your sequence in the right order as you have practiced. You are chaining together all of the specific steps in the sequence. You are floating first to give you time to take longer strokes and maintain your rhythm. Start exhaling 20% of your air before and as you take your first stroke with your breathing side arm. This makes it easier for you to roll your shoulder and head, and open your mouth to inhale air back in.

To help trigger each specific movement, repeat the phrase - **"pull, take a breath, put your head back down, bring your other arm around."** If you still struggle with your timing, then you need to go back and repeat previous steps standing at the wall to master your stroking and breathing.

128 REPEAT FOR 3-5 STROKES TO MASTER YOUR TIMING

Continue to master your breathing while swimming. Repeat the previous step until you can swim five breathing strokes across the shallow end of the pool without having to stop. It's important for you to feel comfortable taking a breath every dominant arm stroke. You need to replace your air supply as you go. It's as natural as breathing when walking.

But unlike a walk, there may be no bottom shallow enough for you to stand up and you must keep going. Yes, you can stop to tread water and float, or you can roll on your back to rest and take a few breaths to recover. When you are efficient, you will not burn up all of your energy. And efficiency comes from mastery of your floating skills to reduce resistance.

129 SWIM WITH YOUR BREATHING ACROSS THE WIDTH OF THE SHALLOW END AND MAINTAIN YOUR RHYTHM SEQUENCE

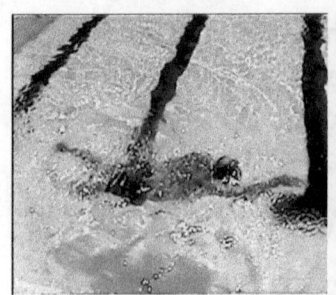  

Prove to yourself that the water depth makes no difference. Swim across the entire width of the shallow end without stopping and take a breath every right arm (dominant arm) stroke. This is your final lead up step to swimming across the corner of the deep end to build your confidence. When you're comfortable swimming on top of the water, it makes no difference how deep it is.

130 SWIM STROKING YOUR BREATHING ARM ONLY WITH YOUR BREATHING AND THEN PRACTICE ON YOUR OTHER SIDE WITH NO BREATHING

You can improve your strength and efficiency by focusing on one arm swimming. Start with your breathing arm, and do your breathing while kicking mostly on your side. Your non stroking arm will stay in the face float position. Then roll to the other side, and practice one arm stroking on that side with no breathing holding your breath. Unlike what I show, roll your shoulders, but don't turn your head when working your non-breathing arm stroke. This will help you to focus on your catch and early rotation to feel the water pressure on your hand and forearm to make better strokes.

Now give yourself or your kid a pat on the back. You have taught yourself how to swim freestyle efficiently. And you can swim continuously without having to stop to breathe. This and your floating skills can help save your life someday.

But please don't stop here. Learn all your strokes, and water safety concerns in unfamiliar places to avoid risks.

Never overestimate your swimming ability. There is always room for improvement.

*****

Now go and invest in another book in my "Teach Yourself To Swim" series.

If you like this book, please tell your friends and write a positive review on Amazon to help save more lives with quality content.

Here is the fast link to your book to write your review on Amazon:

http://www.LearnToSwimProgram.com/Amazon-Reviews